MARTHA ALBERTSON FINEMAN

# VULNERABILITY THEORY AND THE TRINITY LECTURES

Institutionalizing the Individual

First published in Great Britain in 2025 by

Bristol University Press
University of Bristol
1–9 Old Park Hill
Bristol
BS2 8BB
UK
t: +44 (0)117 374 6645
e: bup-info@bristol.ac.uk

Details of international sales and distribution partners are available at
bristoluniversitypress.co.uk

© Bristol University Press 2025

British Library Cataloguing in Publication Data
A catalogue record for this book is available from the British Library

ISBN 978-1-5292-4283-6 hardcover
ISBN 978-1-5292-4284-3 paperback
ISBN 978-1-5292-4285-0 ePub
ISBN 978-1-5292-4286-7 ePdf

The right of Martha Albertson Fineman to be identified as author of this work
has been asserted by her in accordance with the Copyright, Designs and Patents
Act 1988.

All rights reserved: no part of this publication may be reproduced, stored in
a retrieval system, or transmitted in any form or by any means, electronic,
mechanical, photocopying, recording, or otherwise without the prior permission
of Bristol University Press.

Every reasonable effort has been made to obtain permission to reproduce copyrighted
material. If, however, anyone knows of an oversight, please contact the publisher.

The statements and opinions contained within this publication are solely those
of the author and not of the University of Bristol or Bristol University Press.
The University of Bristol and Bristol University Press disclaim responsibility
for any injury to persons or property resulting from any material published in
this publication.

Bristol University Press works to counter discrimination on
grounds of gender, race, disability, age and sexuality.

Cover design: Andrew Corbett
Front cover image: iStock/agsandrew

# Law, Society, Policy

*Series Editor:* **Rosie Harding,**
University of Birmingham

---

Law, Society, Policy offers an outlet for high quality, socio-legal research monographs and edited collections with the potential for policy impact.

## Also available in the series:

*Future Directions in Surrogacy Law*
by **Kirsty Horsey, Zaina Mahmoud**
and **Katherine Wade**

*Adult Social Care Law and Policy*
by **Jean McHale** and **Laura Noszlopy**

*Mental Capacity Law, Sexual Relationships, and Intimacy*
edited by **Beverley Clough** and **Laura Pritchard-Jones**

*Children's Voices, Family Disputes and Child-Inclusive Mediation*
by **Anne Barlow** and **Jan Ewing**

*Observing Justice*
by **Judith Townend** and **Lucy Welsh**

*Egalitarian Digital Privacy*
by **Tsachi Keren-Paz**

*Fragile Rights*
by **Anne Revillard**

*Polygamy, Policy and Postcolonialism in English Marriage Law*
by **Zainab Naqvi**

*Intersex Embodiment*
by **Fae Garland** and **Mitchell Travis**

*Unsettling Apologies*
edited by **Melanie Judge** and **Dee Smythe**

*Death, Family and the Law*
by **Edward Kirton-Darling**

*Deprivation of Liberty in the Shadows of the Institution*
by **Lucy Series**

## Find out more at
bristoluniversitypress.co.uk/law-society-policy

# Law, Society, Policy

*Series Editor:* **Rosie Harding**,
University of Birmingham

## International Advisory Board:

**Dr Lynette Chua**, National University of Singapore, Singapore
**Professor Margaret Davies**, Flinders University, Australia
**Professor Martha Fineman**, Emory University, US
**Professor Marc Hertogh**, University of Groningen, The Netherlands
**Professor Fiona Kelly**, La Trobe University, Melbourne, Australia
**Professor Fiona de Londras**, University of Birmingham, UK
**Dr Anna Mäki-Petäjä-Leinonen**, University of Eastern Finland, Finland
**Professor Ambreena Manji**, Cardiff University, UK
**Professor Linda Mulcahy**, University of Oxford, UK
**Professor Vanessa Munro**, University of Warwick, UK
**Professor Debra Parkes**, University of British Columbia, Canada
**Dr Antu Sorainen**, University of Helsinki, Finland
**Professor Dee Smythe**, University of Cape Town, South Africa
**Professor Michael Thomson**, University of Leeds, UK and University of Technology Sydney, Australia
**Dr Bridgette Toy-Cronin**, University of Otago, New Zealand
**Dr Lisa Vanhala**, University College London, UK

**Find out more at**
bristoluniversitypress.co.uk/law-society-policy

# Contents

| | | |
|---|---|---|
| Series Editor's Preface | | viii |
| Introduction | | 1 |
| one | **Feminist Origins of Vulnerability Theory** | 10 |
| | Introduction to Chapter 1 | 10 |
| | 1.1 Equality | 11 |
| | 1.2 Creating 'separate spheres' – the public and private | 13 |
| |     1.2.1 The gendered constitutional and legal subject | 14 |
| |         1.2.1.1 The exclusionary private domain | 15 |
| |         1.2.1.2 The paradox of equality | 19 |
| | 1.3 Equality achieved | 21 |
| |     1.3.1 Equality in an unequal world | 22 |
| |     1.3.2 Vulnerability Theory and equality | 23 |
| |     1.3.3 Babies and bathwater | 25 |
| | 1.4 Vulnerability Theory – 'existential pragmatism' or 'pragmatic determinism' | 28 |
| two | **Lecture 1 – Reasoning From the Body** | 31 |
| | Introduction to Lecture 1 | 31 |
| | 2.1 The body | 39 |
| | 2.2 Liberty and independence – ignoring the body | 42 |
| | 2.3 Dependence and the embedded vulnerable subject | 44 |
| | 2.4 Conclusion – institutions and interdependence | 47 |
| three | **Lecture 2 – Social Justice** | 53 |
| | Introduction to Lecture 2 | 53 |
| | 3.1 Defining social justice | 58 |

|   |   |   |   |   |
|---|---|---|---|---|
|  | 3.2 | Centring the individual in conceptions of justice | | 61 |
|  | 3.3 | Vulnerability Theory and social justice | | 67 |
|  |  | 3.3.1 Resilience | | 68 |
|  |  | 3.3.2 Social institutions and relationships | | 69 |
|  | 3.4 | Social justice questions from a vulnerability perspective | | 70 |
| four | **Lecture 3 – Injury** | | | **72** |
|  | Introduction to Lecture 3 | | | 72 |
|  | 4.1 | Individual and collective harm | | 75 |
|  | 4.2 | Dependency and injury | | 77 |
|  | 4.3 | Injury and state responsibility | | 82 |
| five | **Lecture 4 – Inevitable Inequality** | | | **90** |
|  | Introduction to Lecture 4 | | | 90 |
|  | 5.1 | The unstable individual – vulnerability and change | | 93 |
|  | 5.2 | Structuring institutional arrangements | | 95 |
|  |  | 5.2.1 State responsibility and institutional construction | | 96 |
|  |  |  | 5.2.1.1 Authoritative or despotic power | 96 |
|  |  |  | 5.2.1.2 Institutional and infrastructural power | 98 |
| six | **Institutionalizing the Individual** | | | **106** |
|  | Introduction to Chapter 6 | | | 106 |
|  | 6.1 | The body | | 107 |
|  | 6.2 | The social and political implications of the universal | | 108 |
|  |  | 6.2.1 The institutionalized individual | | 109 |
|  |  |  | 6.2.1.1 Reframing the individual within social structures | 111 |
|  |  |  | 6.2.1.2 Implications for legal and political theory | 112 |
|  |  | 6.2.2 Biological mandates | | 112 |

|   |   |   |
|---|---|---|
| 6.3 | Collective crises | 115 |
|  | 6.3.1 The US experience – individual over institutional | 116 |
|  | 6.3.2 Vulnerability – mandate or imperative | 118 |

| | |
|---|---|
| Bibliography | 121 |
| Index | 127 |

# Series Editor's Preface

The Law, Society, Policy series publishes high-quality, socio-legal research monographs and edited collections with the potential for policy impact. Cutting across the traditional divides of legal scholarship, Law, Society, Policy offers an interdisciplinary, policy-engaged approach to socio-legal research that explores law in its social and political contexts with a particular focus on the place of law in everyday life.

The series seeks to take an explicitly society-first view of socio-legal studies, with a focus on the ways that law shapes social life, and the constitutive nature of law and society. International in scope, engaging with domestic, international and global legal and regulatory frameworks, texts in the Law, Society, Policy series engage with the full range of socio-legal topics and themes.

# Introduction

In 2022, I was invited by a group of scholars at Trinity College, Dublin to deliver a series of lectures on the concept of vulnerability as the basis for an enhanced vision of state or collective responsibility.[1] I organized the lectures around several principles that highlighted how the insights of what is called 'Vulnerability Theory' reveal and challenge the foundational assumptions underlying mainstream legal and political approaches to justice. My fundamental belief, and the underlying premise of Vulnerability Theory, is that to be appropriately labelled just, a theory must be attentive to the material circumstances[2] of the human condition, emphasizing the interconnectedness and dependence of individuals within society, as well as the complexities of contemporary life.

In viewing such circumstances and complexities as primary considerations, Vulnerability Theory could be deemed an application of Robert Merton's 'theory of the middle range',[3]

---

[1] For more information on the Trinity College lectures and to view the videos, see Trinity Lectures, *Vulnerability, Justice, and the Human Condition* by Prof. Martha A. Fineman, https://vimeo.com/showcase/9966989.

[2] Addressing the material conditions of existence is important because it inevitably leads to a critical examination of the ideological foundations of individualism and the centring of the individual above collective interests that is so prevalent in today's political discourse.

[3] 'Theory of the middle range' is a term developed by the sociologist, Robert K. Merton, in the late 1940s as a way of connecting high-level social theory with empirically observable patterns of everyday life. The emphasis is on trying to understand how concrete realities are shaped by and interpreted through abstract theoretical structures. The interesting questions are found in the tension that inevitably arises between high-level abstract concepts and mundane application of those principles. Looking at the empirical realities can call into question the validity or

which posits that the most significant (and confounding) questions often arise in the tension generated in the spaces between the empirical realities of life and the grand theories or metanarratives of political and public aspirations. These tensions present a challenging and compelling occasion for theoretical, as well as practical, adjustments and revisions.

Vulnerability Theory begins by considering the corporeal body as its foundational empirical concept, focusing on the implications of the fragility and dependency of the body while critically assessing the abstract constructs that dominate our political world, such as equality and liberty, which constrain and limit our vision for change and transformation. By emphasizing the corporeal body, Vulnerability Theory foregrounds the physical and social realities of human existence, advocating for a shift in critical attention (at least initially) from abstract ideals to concrete human experiences. In contrast to 'reasoning from the body'[4] and therefore grappling with its material implications, most contemporary political and legal debates (including those advanced in many critical approaches) are couched in abstract ideals, shaped by eighteenth-century notions of rights that elevate and position the interests of the individual as somehow independent of and disconnected from society and its institutions.

Politicians and policymakers across the ideological spectrum routinely valorize the notion of autonomy, lauding a belief in agency and self-sufficiency.[5] Legislative

---

practical applicability of certain grand ideals and aspirations that dominate approaches to governing, as well as suggesting ways to successfully modify individual and collective behaviour. This approach bridges the gap between grand theories and practical, everyday experiences, aligning well with contemporary demands for institutional and socially responsive legal frameworks. See: Robert K. Merton, *Social Theory and Social Structure* (Free Press 1968).

[4] This is the title and theme of the first lecture.

[5] 'Liberal Democracy', *Encyclopedia.com*, https://www.encyclopedia.com/international/legal-and-political-magazines/liberal-democracy. Liberal democracy is generally understood to be a system of government in which

INTRODUCTION

and judicial constructions of the appropriate relationship between the individual and the state are negotiated within this rhetoric, and both rights-based and social contractarian theories are founded on the illusion of an independent and uncontextualized individual. A corresponding conclusion, which is simultaneously advanced, is that state action is potentially (even likely) abusive: it is certainly not to be considered as in any way routinely required, but rather assumed inconsistent with the wellbeing of the individual.[6] It is this set of assertions about the relationship between the actions of the state and ultimate individual wellbeing that Vulnerability Theory seeks to disrupt.[7] It provides a crucial framework for understanding and addressing the nature and complexity of contemporary societal challenges,

---

people consent to their rulers, and rulers, in turn, are constitutionally constrained to respect individual rights. Liberal democracy owes its origins to particular philosophic doctrines and constitutional developments, which arose especially in England and the US. The adjective 'liberal' points to a set of philosophic doctrines emphasizing human equality that were developed in the early modern period, beginning roughly in the seventeenth century. The emphasis on individual rights and autonomy in eighteenth-century political thought, exemplified by thinkers such as John Locke and Jean-Jacques Rousseau, often overlooks the dependent nature of human beings.

[6] 'Progressive' or 'left' critiques also tend to encapsulate a negative view of the state as abusive, carceral, or punitive, a force to be resisted. Vulnerability Theory seeks to articulate a state responsive to the needs of the individual, one that provides the institutional resources essential for anyone to survive, let alone thrive in society. It also recognizes that, although the state can be captured, compromised, and corrupted, it remains the best option among the many that could feasibly craft and enforce the rules by which we all live our day-to-day lives. These arguments are set out in more detail in the following chapters.

[7] From a philosophical perspective, Vulnerability Theory posits that individual interests must be balanced with collective responsibilities considering the structural conditions that shape opportunities as well as capabilities.

such as pandemics, climate change, and increasing economic inequality.

Vulnerability Theory grew out of feminist-based approaches to legal policy and reform first associated with the family.[8] As the family is the societal institution primarily responsible for children, the elderly, and others in need of care, family law and policy has had to be attentive to the realities of the corporeal body and their implications. This feminist foundation emphasizes the importance of placing care and dependency as central and primary themes in crafting legal and social policy. Feminist concern with family caretaking focused attention beyond the needs of specific individuals to also examine the complex social and legal institutional arrangements necessary for societal, as well as individual and family, survival. Vulnerability Theory recognizes that, while these arrangements may be understood as constituting gender-based injustice, they are more accurately and productively first viewed as arrangements that affect everyone in society that very well may have negative, universal negative consequences even if aggravated by gender. By addressing the *systemic* nature of family arrangements, what have been understood as gender injustices can be productively approached instead as indicating a need for comprehensive *institutional* reforms. From a Vulnerability Theory perspective, an institutional approach is necessary. Mundane social institutions, such as the family, are the structural realities of everyone's everyday lives, defining the frameworks for our lived experience and profoundly shaping our expectations, options, aspirations, and opportunities.

---

[8] The feminist origins of Vulnerability Theory are deeply rooted in critiques of traditional family law and policy. For a comprehensive overview, see Martha Albertson Fineman, *The Neutered Mother, The Sexual Family and Other Twentieth Century Tragedies* (Routledge 2014).

INTRODUCTION

## Organization of this volume

Chapter 1 addresses the feminist foundations of Vulnerability Theory, particularly as they are grounded in understanding the position of the family. The next four chapters are based on the (slightly edited for clarity) transcripts of the individual Trinity lectures. Each is also annotated in order to provide some insight into the evolution of Vulnerability Theory over the past decade. Some of these explanatory footnotes also address certain misunderstandings or difficulties that some readers have had with the very idea and meaning of the concept of vulnerability, particularly the resistance that often arises to its implications for social policy.

### *First lecture – 'Reasoning From the Body'*

Lecture 1 (Chapter 2) develops the foundational concept of the universal or ontological body. It supports the preliminary theoretical assertion of Vulnerability Theory that because we are *embodied* (and therefore vulnerable) beings, humans are inevitably *embedded* in (and dependent upon) social institutions and relationships throughout the life course. This inevitable reliance on social arrangements is further posited as the impetus for us as a species to come together in families, communities, to form political organizations, both locally and internationally. Vulnerability, understood as a key impetus for the creation of society and its institutions, must also be central in the political process of defining our notions of state or collective responsibility, as well as judging what social arrangements are essential for individual and societal wellbeing.

### *Second lecture – 'Social Justice'*

Lecture 2 (Chapter 3) begins by asking the provocative question: what do we mean when we talk about *social* justice? The emphasis is on understanding the *social* or institutional and structural notion of justice in contrast to justice claims focusing on correcting or adjusting a situation perceived to be inequitable for some individuals or particular groups, as in racial or gender justice, or in regard to a particular form of imbalance, such as economic justice. The assertion is that social justice should be considered a universal and inclusive task in contrast to the individualistic rights-based or social contract frameworks currently favoured. In this regard, a social justice perspective would take into account the complete range and complexity of everyone's interest in fashioning institutions and relationships: the collective particular interests of the various individuals and groups, as well as the broader and more inclusive interests of the community and society more generally, would then be considered in the initial design of fundamental social institutions.[9]

### Third lecture – 'Injury'

Lecture 3 (Chapter 4) reframes the notion of injury to incorporate neglect or the failure of the state to act in the face of persistent inequalities or injustices. It recognizes that conceptions of injury that primarily focus on the individual in terms of either intent or harm are not sufficient to achieve social justice as it was clarified and explained in Lecture 1. In moving beyond an individually focused examination of the nature of injury, this chapter also challenges the liberal or libertarian principle that frames state intervention as presumptively injurious.[10]

---

[9] The concept of social justice as described here emphasizes the importance of designing societal structures that inherently promote fairness, accommodation, and equity. This perspective seeks to integrate a holistic view of justice that encompasses economic, social, and political dimensions, ensuring that all members of society can participate fully and fairly in its benefits and responsibilities.

[10] This reconceptualization of injury aligns with philosophical critiques of negative liberty, highlighting the essential role of positive state actions

Not surprisingly, a Vulnerability Theory conception of injury builds on the basic realization that we inevitably live our lives dependent on social institutions and relationships that are inescapably shaped by law and legal principles: intervention or governance is not only inevitable but essential for the wellbeing of society as well as the individual. From both a practical and an ethical or moral perspective, this dependency demands the formation of principles and policies of governmental responsibility ensuring institutional integrity and implementing policies designed to foster social justice.[11] This approach to what constitutes injury resonates in the words of Elie Wiesel, who wisely reflected: 'The opposite of love is not hate, it's indifference. The opposite of art is not ugliness, it's indifference. The opposite of faith is not heresy, it's indifference. And the opposite of life is not death, it's indifference.'[12] Vulnerability Theory asks us to consider indifference as a profound injury, one that demands the crafting of a remedy of caring and concern and a state with policies that are responsive to the human condition of vulnerability and its inevitable reality of institutional dependency.

## *Fourth lecture – 'Inevitable Inequality'*

Lecture 4 (Chapter 5) presents what may be one of the most significant insights from understanding Vulnerability

---

in achieving justice and equality. The idea that state inaction can itself constitute a form of injury necessitates a profound re-evaluation of governmental responsibilities and the ethical imperatives underlying social justice.

[11] This redefinition of injury aligns with critiques of the state as a neutral entity, underscoring the state's active role in perpetuating or alleviating inequality. A critical examination of the state's responsibilities is necessary to address systemic injustices and the conditions that give rise to them.

[12] Elie Wiesel as quoted in *US News and World Report*, October 27, 1986.

Theory: inequality is inevitable. As is generally true with Vulnerability Theory, the basis for this insight, as well as its implications, require us to move away from an exclusive focus on the individual to consider the institutional relationships that are essential in shaping the material and normative terms of our very existence.

It is within the contexts and confines of these essential institutions that we live our lives, adopting and inhabiting the social identities that correspond to institutional purpose and design. These social identities are relational, typically the products of historic political and cultural forces. Determined in the first place by the form and function of the social institution in which they are found, they are typically forged in complementary relational terms, reflecting the necessity of unequal levels of dependency and the need for unequal assignments of responsibility. Examples of such inevitable and appropriate inequality are found in relationships such as those of parent/child within the family, employer/employee within the workplace, and doctor/patient within the healthcare system.

This chapter asserts that we have not successfully articulated a way to think about how to achieve justice in both institutional and asymmetric or unequal terms. To do so would require leaving the individual and particularized situations behind (at least temporarily) and considering the initial questions inherent in designing social institutions. This approach, however, requires that we recognize vulnerability and dependency as requiring a robust sense of state responsibility.

### *Chapter 6 – 'Institutionalizing the Individual'*

Chapter 6 expands on the suggestion (or aspiration) contained in the subtitle for this volume: 'Institutionalizing the Individual'. It brings together some of the insights from the lectures, suggesting how they might productively be applied to some contemporary collective challenges that are not readily addressed using current dominant theoretical constructs,

constructs that have isolated the individual from the realities of vulnerability and dependency.

## Acknowledgements

I would like to thank the two Vulnerability and the Human Condition Initiative postdoctoral fellows, Helena Moradi and Bojan Perovic, and the Initiative's wonderful program coordinator, Mangala Kanayson, for their support and encouragement, as well as their invaluable assistance with finalizing this manuscript. The generosity of these three very talented individuals made the process of completing this project not only easier, but more enjoyable.

# ONE

# Feminist Origins of Vulnerability Theory[1]

## Introduction to Chapter 1

This chapter traces the feminist origins of Vulnerability Theory, considering how some early feminist legal critiques by focusing on the social institution of the family also laid the groundwork for a more comprehensive understanding of equality and social justice. The family is a fundamental social institution, which performs a range of socially essential tasks. Those tasks historically have been allocated based on the construction of gender differences. This chapter suggests that, in bringing the gendered family within a gender-equality (or neutrality) paradigm, reformers erred in focusing too much on gender discrimination or disadvantage and not enough on the need to reallocate the necessary dependency work that must be done to replicate society across a wider range of social institutions.

---

[1] The Feminism and Legal Theory (FLT) Project at Emory University, celebrating its 40th anniversary in 2024, has been pivotal in examining how law and culture shape gender-related expectations, policies, and practices. The FLT archives, housed at MacMillan Law Library, contain valuable resources for feminist research and the history of feminist legal theory. The FLT Project has also led to the Vulnerability and the Human Condition Initiative, which advances a social justice framework based on human vulnerability and the need for a responsive state. For more information, see https://law.emory.edu/centers-and-programs/feminism-and-legal-theory-project.html.

By framing the issue primarily as one of individual rights and gender equality, reformers left unexamined the structural inequities that persisted in the allocation of caregiving duties. The failure to challenge the underlying assumption that the family is the primary and 'natural' institution responsible for managing dependency left intact a system that continues to rely heavily on unpaid or underpaid caregiving labour.

This chapter contends that the feminist legal reformers' pursuit of gender equality, while a necessary step in the quest for social justice, was incomplete. Vulnerability Theory advances the social justice project by offering a more comprehensive framework that recognizes the universality of human dependency and calls for a redistribution of the burdens of care across all of society. This approach not only challenges the public/private divide that has historically confined care work to the family but also urges a reconfiguration of institutional arrangements to ensure that caregiving is recognized, supported, and fairly distributed.

★★★

## 1.1 Equality

Equality was articulated as an important principle in the eighteenth-century foundational documents expressing the governmental philosophy of the US.[2] However, as has been

---

[2] These documents, influenced by Enlightenment thinkers such as John Locke and Jean-Jacques Rousseau, emphasized individual rights and the social contract as the basis for political legitimacy. The Declaration of Independence asserts that 'all men are created equal', yet this notion of natural rights and Rousseau's concept of the general will underpin the principles of liberty and equality in these documents. However, these ideals were inherently limited by the social and cultural norms of their time and did not extend to women. Similarly, the US Constitution originally did not address the equality of women.

repeatedly pointed out, at the time those equality-celebrating documents were drafted, there was widespread acceptance of the idea that equality was a qualified concept. It was widely accepted that there were significant fundamental differences between certain classes of men, as well as between men and women that logically and legally meant equality was far from a universal principle.[3] These distinctions were not merely political but were deeply embedded in the legal frameworks and institutions of the time, reinforcing a hierarchical social order.

From a legal philosophical perspective, this qualified notion of equality reflects a fundamental tension within liberal political theory: the conflict between universal principles and contextual applications. This tension is evident in the way legal systems have historically constructed and enforced hierarchies (based on categories such as race, gender, and class). This notion of fundamental differences, with some men occupying a position of political and legal privilege or natural advantage, had institutional implications. Societal arrangements such as that of master/servant (and, of course, slavery)[4] or the family, incorporated hierarchical relationships among different groups. Any potential incongruity between governing ideal and structural reality was resolved (or obscured) by the creation of what should be considered as separate legal or constitutional subjectivities for different categories of citizens. Grand constitutional principles such as equality and liberty were to govern the relationship between the state and those considered to be full citizens, while the

---

[3] Sex was not the only designated category of constitutionally relevant difference. Markers of economic status, such as property ownership were also used to justify different rules of constitutional protection and participation for many within society. A form of inferior constitutional status still applies to children.

[4] Shamefully, the institution of slavery eluded any notions of individual entitlement or rights for the slave. Under the Slave Codes that governed slavery, enslaved persons were considered property, not persons: https://www.britannica.com/topic/slave-code.

state's responsibility to subordinate individuals was considered appropriately governed by different standards. One manifestation of this distinction between the state's relationship to full versus subordinate citizens was the conceptual divide created between the public and private spheres or arenas of life.

## 1.2 Creating 'separate spheres' – the public and private

Within the political and economic realms, women were cast as incapable of full or effective participation in the rigours and challenges of public life. They were considered appropriately situated politically within a special domestic domain that was designed to reflect the needs of their peculiar status.[5] Women's 'natural' dependence mandated they be secured within the patriarchal family, which would compensate for their perceived inferior attributes. The idea was that women could successfully achieve their societal role if and when they were firmly under the control (or guidance) of their fathers and husbands. Significantly, the state's responsibility for women as citizens was not ignored or side-stepped by this patriarchal placement. Indeed, women were being treated as 'special' – in need of additional protection, which would be provided by being suitably sheltered from the harshness of public life within the mediating institution of the family.

Neither the exclusion of women from public life nor their special status within the family was considered inappropriate discrimination or exclusion in the negative sense we think of those terms today. Rather, politicians and policymakers designated a neutral, even protective, category or classification, which was justified by reference to contemporary scientific and medical opinions.[6] Notably, this secondary status also did not

---

[5] See the opinions in *Bradwell* and *Mueller* mentioned later in this chapter.

[6] Also, these scientific and medical justifications often relied on biased and flawed research that reinforced existing stereotypes and prejudices. For instance, nineteenth-century medical texts frequently portrayed women

mean that women were not valued as important members of and contributors to society. Women were deemed to have a unique and indispensable societal role in regard to the essential tasks of reproduction and raising the next generation. Those roles, although deemed domestic, were recognized as essential to the continuation of society. They were indispensable complements to the economic and authoritarian roles that men performed within the family as husbands and fathers (wage-earners and disciplinarians).[7]

In this way, the constitutional scheme setting forth separate legal subjectivity for women aligned biological sex with a set of socially imposed gender practices and prohibitions, formally institutionalizing them within the legal construct of the family. The laws and policies that created the family provided the rules that governed both women and men within their family roles, while at the same time establishing the state's interest in and authority over the family, which was understood as a social institution with an essential role in the reproduction of society. The state's involvement in regulating family life reflected broader social and political efforts to maintain an efficient and 'natural' method of societal reproduction.[8]

### *1.2.1 The gendered constitutional and legal subject*

Early US Supreme Court constitutional decisions engrained – even celebrated – this form of gender differentiation and

---

as inherently weaker and more prone to hysteria, justifying their exclusion from many professional and public roles.

[7] This division of roles reinforced the public/private dichotomy, shaping legal and social norms that persisted well into the twentieth century.

[8] For example, coverture laws in nineteenth-century US structured property relations such that married women could not own property independently of their husbands. Similarly, the exclusion of women from voting until the passage of the Nineteenth Amendment in 1920 institutionalized gendered political participation.

specialization. Different treatment under law was considered appropriate given the asserted status-determining biological and social differences between women and men. The uniqueness of the social role for the female sex justified, even compelled, a regulatory regime that carved out separate expectations and expressed distinct gendered legal subjectivities.

*1.2.1.1 The exclusionary private domain*

The justification for the solicitous attention women received in the private sphere of the family also supported their protection from the public. This protection was essential to preserve and guard her natural, divine destiny, which was as mother and wife to serve in the nursery and home. The most notorious expression of this sentiment is found in an 1872 concurring opinion by Justice Bradley in *Bradwell v Illinois:*

> [T]he civil law, as well as nature herself, has always recognized a wide difference in the respective spheres and destinies of man and woman. Man is, or should be, woman's protector and defender. The natural and proper timidity and delicacy which belongs to the female sex evidently unfits it for many of the occupations of civil life. The constitution of the family organization, which is founded in the divine ordinance, as well as in the nature of things, indicates the domestic sphere as that which properly belongs to the domain and functions of womanhood. The harmony, not to say identity, of interests and views which belong, or should belong, to the family institution is repugnant to the idea of a woman adopting a distinct and independent career from that of her husband. So firmly fixed was this sentiment in the founders of the common law that it became a maxim of that system of jurisprudence that a woman had no legal existence separate from her husband, who

was regarded as her head and representative in the social state.[9]

The acceptance of the idea, articulated in *Bradwell*, that naturally there must be a distinct gender-based legal subject was also found in a variety of other Supreme Court pronouncements. For example, the Court in *Muller v Oregon* (1908) opined that women were decidedly different from (and weaker than) men in upholding Progressive era labour legislation monitoring the hours that women (but not men) employed in factories and laundries could work. As the unanimous opinion stated:

> That woman's physical structure and the performance of maternal functions place her at a disadvantage in the struggle for subsistence is obvious. This is especially true

---

[9] *Bradwell v State of Illinois*, 83 US 130 (1872) 141. This sentiment can be contextualized within the broader intellectual currents. Justice Bradley's concurrence can be analyzed as an embodiment of the social contract theories advanced by Hobbes, Locke, and Rousseau. While these theories emphasized individual rights, they often marginalized women by confining them to the private sphere. The nineteenth century witnessed the consolidation of the separate spheres ideology, which posited that men and women occupied fundamentally different domains – men in the public sphere of work and politics, and women in the private sphere of home and family. This ideology was reinforced by contemporary interpretations of natural law and theological doctrines used to justify the legal and social subordination of women. Influential thinkers such as John Locke, who highlighted property and paternal authority, and Jean-Jacques Rousseau, who advocated distinct educational paths for boys and girls based on their 'natural' roles, played a significant role in this context. Rousseau's *Emile* (1762), for instance, presented a vision of women's roles confined to domesticity and nurturing, which profoundly influenced legal and social norms. Furthermore, the cultural narrative that reinforced this legal perspective is also reflected in literature; Henrik Ibsen's *A Doll's House* ([1879] 1992) critiques the stifling domestic roles imposed on women and the lack of personal agency available to them within the family structure.

when the burdens of motherhood are upon her. Even when they are not, by abundant testimony of the medical fraternity continuance for a long time on her feet at work, repeating this from day to day, tends to injurious effects upon the body, and as healthy mothers are essential to vigorous offspring, the physical well-being of woman becomes an object of public interest and care in order to preserve the strength and vigor of the race.[10]

The brief in *Muller* built on the idea of separate constitutional status for women, devoting hundreds of pages to the proposition that the state had an interest in protecting the health of women. The importance of women's societal role as mothers was sufficient to justify the state's limiting their liberty of contract, even if it could not do so in regard to men.[11] Women, it was argued, were physically and emotionally different, as were their natural roles in society, therefore justifying special legal protection.

---

[10] *Muller v State of Oregon*, 208 US 412 (1908) 421. The late nineteenth and early twentieth centuries were marked by a significant interest in social Darwinism and biological determinism, which frequently served as a pseudo-scientific justification for gender discrimination. The notion that women's reproductive functions constrained their physical and intellectual abilities was widely accepted and propagated by prominent figures such as Dr Edward Clarke. His 1873 book, *Sex in Education*, argued that higher education could impair women's health and reproductive capacity. These perspectives were not isolated but were part of a broader cultural and intellectual milieu, including eugenics, that perpetuated beliefs in inherent racial and gender hierarchies.

[11] The gender-specific approach taken by progressive reformers in *Muller* was influenced by the earlier case of *Lochner v New York* (1905), in which the court rejected state efforts to limit working hours, citing 'liberty of contract'. In *Lochner*, the majority opinion stated that the law did not affect public safety, morals, or welfare (53–7). By contrast, *Muller* legislation targeted women specifically, justifying protection based on assumed gender differences and invoking state interest and public purpose to support police power regulation.

At this time that these protective labour provisions were advanced, women were also organizing and advocating for the right to vote.[12] The *New York Times* on February 28, 1908, noted what it thought to be apparent contradictions in the two movements (protective labour legislation and suffrage), which both raised the question of women's equality. Noting the arguments for special, differential (and unequal) treatment in the *Muller* decision, the *Times* stated: 'We leave to the advocates of women suffrage to say whether this decision makes for, or against, the success of their cause.'[13]

Media cynicism aside, it should be noted that, in spite of the gendered wording justifying the outcome in *Muller*, many reformers at that time were also deeply concerned with the conditions under which men laboured. While organizations such as the National Consumers' League and the National Women's Trade Union League may have been comfortable for strategic and practical reasons with taking advantage of the prevalent bias that women workers were more delicate and easily exploited than their male counterparts, they also anticipated that such regulations could work as a wedge, opening up a way to rethink the employment relationship more generally, eventually moving toward successful legislation gaining protections for all workers.[14] Protections for male workers were not to become viable until the 1930s when the judiciary became more deferential to legislatures in the wake of

---

[12] Amendment XIX, granting women suffrage, came into effect on August 18, 1920.

[13] Cited in 'The Position of Woman', *The New York Times*, February 26, 1908.

[14] See: David E. Bernstein, 'Lochner's Feminist Legacy' (2003) 101 *Michigan Law Review* 1960 notes that these reform organizations used protective legislation for women as a strategic approach to push for broader labour reforms. These organizations recognized that, while the immediate focus was on women, the ultimate goal was to improve working conditions for all labourers.

the reformatory zeal of the New Deal. By that time, however, the notion of women needing additional special protections due to their domestic role and general physical and emotional sensitivities was ensconced in American jurisprudence, not to be uprooted until the 1960s and 1970s when the Equal Protection Clause and Title VII were used to impose gender neutrality as the preferred legal norm.[15]

### 1.2.1.2 The paradox of equality

*Muller* is an interesting case from the perspective of contemporary legal theory in that it can be viewed as raising issues of the relationship between equality and more expansive concepts of social justice. On the one hand, the regulations at issue in *Muller* addressed the real-world circumstances of many women, particularly working-class women, who desperately (even if not uniquely) needed protections from oppressive and exploitative workplaces. On the other hand, to justify reforms by arguing that they were warranted by specific gender differences risked reinforcing and reifying the existing anti-gender-equality bias that reinforced the idea of a gendered legal subjectivity. Paradoxically, either approach implicitly enshrined the normative legal subject as gendered male.[16] Some Progressive reformers felt a partial (gendered)

---

[15] See Gretchen Ritter, *The Constitution as Social Design: Gender and Civic Membership in the American Constitutional Order* (Stanford University Press 2006) discusses how the 1960s and 1970s, inspired by the civil rights movement, saw significant legislative and judicial advances for women. This period marked a shift towards gender neutrality, challenging the entrenched societal beliefs about inherent sex differences and traditional gender roles. However, the author notes that the commitment to gender equality was often ambivalent, reflecting the complexities and limitations in fully addressing sex and gender issues during this transformative period.

[16] This is the case because, on the one hand, women would be seen as different, lesser and weaker (separate constitutional subjects), while treating them the same as men ignored that they had an unequal and

victory was at least a step forward on the long road toward humane labour reforms.

From a pragmatic perspective, even if imperfect and incomplete, such reforms helped improve the real-life circumstances of women who were considered to be among the most oppressed workers. The feminist reformers who strongly believed that, in the long run, it is essential to fight for an uncompromised version of equality that would require women to be treated the same as men argued that the pragmatic approach by emphasizing gender difference inevitably would solidify and even exacerbate the general sexist tendencies found in society. They foresaw that this pragmatic choice would likely be used against women in the workplace and elsewhere. It is undeniable that these predictions were accurate in the years that followed. The logic of *Muller* was used by courts to validate laws that confined women to low-paying jobs or precluded them from working overtime.[17] Women were even barred for protective reasons from holding certain higher paid traditionally male jobs, such as bartender[18] or mailman, and from working in dangerous places like foundries or mines.[19]

These sorts of exclusionary outcomes as a result of conceding gender differences were a major motivation for the liberal legal feminist reformers in the mid-twentieth century, who advocated for a formal or sameness of treatment approach

---

socially imposed set of burdens that made performance and participation in the workplace even more difficult and detrimental (ideal worker based on male-gendered norms).

[17] *Bosley v McLaughlin*, 236 US 385 (1915) 394; *Ex parte Hawley* (1911) 40, aff'd *Hawley v Walker*, 232 US 718 (1914) 718; *Miller v Wilson*, 236 US 373 (1915) 379–80.

[18] See *Goesaert v Cleary*, 335 US 464 (1948), where the Supreme Court upheld a Michigan law that prohibited women from working as bartenders unless they were the wife or daughter of the male owner of the establishment.

[19] Alice Kessler-Harris, *Out to Work: A History of Wage-Earning Women in the United States* (Oxford University Press 1982) 201–5.

to equality. They rejected the notion that there were any *legally relevant* gender differences, an argument that ultimately prevailed at the Supreme Court level in the 1971 case of *Reed v Reed*.[20] The court held that a statutory preference for men as executors of estates was inconsistent with the Equal Protection Clause of the US Constitution. Arguments that a mandatory sex preference was appropriate and merely adopted for efficiency reasons and to eliminate the need for hearings on the merits, which were argued to be contentiously disruptive of family relations, were rejected. The court found that the gender preference was the very kind of arbitrary legislative choice forbidden by the Equal Protection Clause of the Fourteenth Amendment.[21]

## 1.3 Equality achieved

In twenty-first century industrialized democracies, thanks mostly to feminist reformers, women are no longer legally defined by reproductive roles or family status but are recognized as full and equal constitutional subjects. Even within the family (which historically is the most gender-specific of social institutions), equality – at least for the spouses – is now the guiding principle. We now live in a world in which (at least judging from the legal landscape) equality has vanquished gender discrimination and exclusion. In fact, not only do women now have full constitutional subjectivity, but reforms of family law have had androgynous implications: constitutionally guided family laws have transformed husbands and wives into 'spouses' and fathers and mothers into 'parents' and there have been marked improvements in regard to women's social,

---

[20] 404 US 71 (1971).
[21] Ruth Bader Ginsburg litigated *Reed* for the Women's Rights Project of the ACLU and also took a lead in many of the gender equality cases that followed.

economic, and political equality. It is important to recognize the progress such gender neutrality represents, as well as to respect and celebrate the efforts of those who worked so hard to achieve it. However, not all is ideal, nor has equality proved to always be progress.

### 1.3.1 Equality in an unequal world

Despite the impressive successes in pursuing gender equality, some feminist legal scholars argue that there are significant and costly constraints and limitations inherent in an approach that assumes neutrality or equality is possible, or even desirable. The argument is that delegitimation of sex discrimination has not resulted in real equality between the sexes, noting that, even in situations of formal neutrality, structural bias or unconscious discrimination related to sex stereotypes continues unaddressed, even undetected to the disadvantage of women.

Such arguments may point to the continuing differences between the social and cultural experiences of women and men, while others also note there are experiential and other differences among women that may render gender a less relevant category for analysis when it comes to equality. The continuation of gender-skewed patterns of behaviour, it is argued, reflects the reality that the problems in implementing a regime of sex equality are much more complicated than anticipated by earlier reformers. It is suggested that what we need is a more nuanced notion of equality, one that can be sensitive to gender differences, whether those differences are based on biological distinctiveness or social circumstances. This approach has been described as an attempt to 'put women *into* the Constitution on female rather than male terms'[22] However,

---

[22] Joan Hoff, *Law, Gender, and Injustice: A Legal History of US Women* (NYU Press 1991) 374. This approach aims to achieve gender equity ('equality in sameness') by recognizing differences ('equality in difference'). Vulnerability Theory argues for a more universal approach and seeks to

it seems problematic that, in trying to incorporate continuing social or cultural experiences into policy or legal outcomes, we are also implicitly conceding the appropriateness of having distinct political and legal subjectivities.

### 1.3.2 Vulnerability Theory and equality

Vulnerability Theory takes the implications of an unfinished gender equality revolution seriously. However, as the subsequent lectures will show, it does so not by seeking adjustments within the traditional individualistic approach to rights and responsibilities. A vulnerability framework also does not fracture the legal and political subject based on gender (or other) differences, whether they are argued to be imposed by societal structures and aspirations or biology. Instead, Vulnerability Theory is based on the assertion that there must be a universal legal subject, one that reflects the collective reality of the human condition in all its variants and varieties. It is that universal subject that must be considered in assessing the laws and policies that define the institutional arrangements and structures in which we all live our day-to-day lives and that, in allocating the benefits and burdens inherent in any society, ultimately shape our individual and collective destinies.[23]

Instead of beginning with an anti-discrimination analysis using demographic categories (like male and female), a vulnerability approach would first assess the justice of the

---

ensure that state policies and laws address the underlying and universal vulnerabilities shared by all individuals. See Martha Albertson Fineman, 'Vulnerability and Inevitable Inequality' (2017) 4(3) *Oslo Law Review* 133–49.

[23] In rejecting reliance on the anti-discrimination model of a traditional equality analysis, Vulnerability Theory also sensibly asks what are the benefits or advantages for an individual or group of being included within a fundamentally flawed institutional structure. It also recognizes that sometimes a universal approach also remedies (or at least alters) the problems that particular individuals or groups might be experiencing.

institutional arrangements. This means focusing on examining how institutions that shape the realities of everyday life for everyone, such as the family, workplace, and government more generally, are conceived and designed. This would represent a very different starting place for analysis than the current tendency to confine critical attention to emphasize instances of institutional malfunctioning in regard to specific individuals or groups.

One advantage of such a universal, institutional focus would be that the public/private spheres paradigm that currently bifurcates public policy discussions would dissolve. For example, in considering the family/work conflict so important in earlier feminist discussions, an initial task would be to seriously (and critically) look at the existing allocation of responsibility for societal reproduction among a wide range of social institutions, whether they are now occupying the private or family sphere or not. Such a consideration would certainly implicate those institutions currently considered public, such as those defining the workplace or arrangements within the purview of the state or government.

If we begin with an institutional analysis, we see that existing arrangements are skewed toward the private, with the family primarily bearing the burdens of social reproduction, even though it is all of society that benefits (in fact is dependent upon) that labour. While the family is essential to the successful functioning of other social arrangements, it is largely absent as a serious factor in discussions about what policies and principles should be applied to the 'free' market or various other institutional constructs.

The family is what we might call an 'assumed' institution – somehow naturally evolved to fulfil its essential function even if not accommodated and supported by the policies that have produced market, state and other arenas. It is important in considering how to structure society in a just manner that we do not continue to make this fundamental conceptual error.

### 1.3.3 Babies and bathwater[24]

In some ways we have failed to fully comprehend the lessons that should have been learned from the struggles with implementing gender equality. We continue to locate the problem as an individual or group failure to achieve equality within a social institution, be it the family, the market, or politics – a problem of discrimination (in outcome, if not intent). We tend to focus on the position of the individual, not on the structure and functioning of the institution and its implications for *every* individual,[25] as well as the organization and functioning of society more generally. Focusing on the position of the individual can obscure the extent and nature of the more systemic or practical issues that are embedded in the design and expectations we have established for an institution.[26]

Specifically, regarding family law reform, the problem is much more complicated than the concept of discrimination can capture. In a world that aspires to have gender equality, the allocation of responsibility for a fundamental society-preserving task like caretaking cannot be confined to a mislabelled private family. Otherwise, all the reform has done is to only formally and symbolically liberate individual women from historically predetermined sex roles within a family structure that cannot accommodate such a transformation. The essential social

---

[24] This is a reference to the old saying warning us not to 'throw the baby out with the bathwater' in considering making fundamental changes. I use it here in regard to the past tendency to discard old ideas about traditional family functioning (such as when moving to a gender-neutral or equally model) without considering how to preserve what may continue to be valuable (necessary and viable) within that to be discarded model.

[25] These institutions affect everyone's day-to-day existence, forming the infrastructure for our lives.

[26] The design of the institution and the treatment of the individual are, of course, intimately related. The issue is where (or with what) we begin to frame our questions and seek solutions and how we subsequently imagine and focus our reform energy and aspirations.

reproduction functions that were previously determined along gendered lines have not disappeared.

What was needed was not only the end of the explicitly gendered family and formally allowing the incorporation of previously excluded individuals into the public spheres of life, but a profound transformation of the interdependent infrastructural arrangements of the entire society. The assumed family (in both what were considered its essential form and function) had to be critically examined in the light of shifting expectations about gender equality. This assessment of necessity would include a consideration of how, given changing aspirations and expectations, society should justly allocate institutional and individual responsibility for social reproduction across a variety of social institutions, including the workplace and social welfare systems. In other words, effective and just reform of any social institutions, especially the family, cannot be effectively achieved by merely decreeing there was now to be equality among individuals acting within an unreformed societal institution and incompatible social arrangements – an institution and arrangements that were in fact structured in reliance on gender inequality.

There are specific examples of policies that begin to reflect what sorts of social policy would be successful in responding to dependency and vulnerability. Recognizing the necessity for integrating the roles and functions of various societal institutions, Nordic countries have introduced paternity leave policies, showing significant progress in redefining gender roles within the family and promoting a more equitable sharing of caregiving responsibilities. Additionally, universal access to early childhood education in countries like France and Germany highlights how state support can relieve the family of some of its traditional burdens, leading to better outcomes for both parents and children, as well as society. Further, policies that support flexible hours and job-sharing can help balance work and family responsibilities, reducing the pressure on any single family member to conform to traditional gender roles. Moreover, robust social welfare programmes, such as guaranteed minimum income and affordable housing, can provide families with the financial stability needed to manage caregiving responsibilities and reduce the stress associated with economic precarity.[27]

The need for this kind of fundamental structural reassessment is particularly important when it comes to political ideology and aspiration. It is imperative that we not only recognize but embrace the realities of human vulnerability and social dependency, as well as the necessity (inevitability) of governmental or collective responsibility in constructing our governing political and legal theories and principles. We seem to be unable to escape the past.

The idea of separate spheres and the relegation of women to a distinct domestic sphere where they were assigned unique responsibilities for raising the young and taking care of the developmental, dependency, and caretaking needs of family members enabled eighteenth-century political and legal theorists to avoid a whole range of crucial human experiences in spinning out their grand theories of justice. To these classical theorists, the domestic was not deemed a primary – or even an appropriate – arena for governmental or constitutional concern. Dependency and other uncomfortable aspects of domesticity were not incorporated into the considerations or deliberations of the framers in determining how to position the individual vis-à-vis the state in terms of liberty or equality. They did not form part of the dilemmas contemplated regarding the complexities of the individual in relation to society and its institutions or how to frame rights and assign responsibilities. In other words, the exclusion of the domestic (and its relegation

---

[27] I do not mean to suggest that these policies are in and of themselves sufficient, but only that they are at least designed to pursue an institutional, rather than merely an individualized and particularized, solution to the dilemmas presented by dependency and vulnerability.

to women) and the creation of the allegory of separate spheres facilitated and legitimated the exclusion of a whole range of fundamental human experiences from public or constitutional concern. This resulted in a distortion in the ways we even today articulate and understand the individual in relation to the societal or collective, but also how the legal or constitutional subject is defined.

## 1.4 Vulnerability Theory – 'existential pragmatism' or 'pragmatic determinism'

Vulnerability Theory is grounded in the realization that law and policy cannot be built on theoretical premises and policies that ignore the existential nature of human existence. There are important lessons and profound insights into the human condition that have been obscured by the separation of the family from so-called public (or political) life. It is imperative that we confront the realities and implications of vulnerability and dependency and their implications. A logical place to begin to do so is with the reconfiguration of the legal and political subject. As Lecture 1 demonstrates, Vulnerability Theory does this by reasoning from the body as a foundational theoretical premise.[28]

The premise is that we have continued to ignore what the family (or separate spheres) historically obscured – the human condition of vulnerability mandates social care, accommodation, subsidies, and support – a need that extends beyond the institution of the family to affect our ability to thrive in the larger society. Whether those needs are met affects not only the wellbeing of the individual, but the ultimate success of society itself. Instead, by ignoring dependency

---

[28] See Martha Albertson Fineman, 'Reasoning from the Body: Universal Vulnerability and Social Justice' in Chris Dietz, Michael A. Thomson, and Mitchell Travis (eds), *A Jurisprudence of the Body* (Springer 2020).

and vulnerability, our sense of appropriate state response to injustice has been limited. Our notions of equality and justice are comfortably and narrowly focused on questions of impermissible discrimination. Concepts such as the distinction between negative and positive rights and fear of constraints on individual liberty and autonomy make it difficult to articulate a coherent theory of state responsibility responsive to basic human needs. We glorify the individual, idealizing contract and choice in ways that mask perpetuating injustice by ignoring the realities and social implications of human vulnerability. This approach overlooks the critical insight that vulnerabilities are inherent to the human condition and cannot be addressed through individual effort alone.[29]

We are embodied, fragile beings. As such, we are inevitably and inescapably dependent on institutional structures and relationships throughout our lives. This is the reality that defines the existential nature of the human condition. That reality demands a thoughtful, comprehensive, and pragmatic response on the part of those individuals and institutions that govern the legal, as well as the economic, political, and cultural arrangements in which we inevitably live our everyday lives. Vulnerability Theory has begun to explore what is necessary to achieve such a 'responsive state'. It asks how the reality of human vulnerability and the inevitability of institutional dependence should inform the structures and aspirations for governance, particularly in regard to contextualizing such currently abstracted ideals as liberty, autonomy, independence, and equality. This reconsideration of the legal subject is necessary for the implementation of policies such as universal healthcare or comprehensive and egalitarian educational reform. We must challenge the foundational assumptions of liberal legalism to ensure an expansive and inclusive form of

---

[29] See Martha Albertson Fineman, 'The Vulnerable Subject and the Responsive State' (2010) 60 *Emory Law Journal* 251.

social justice.[30] At a minimum, our legal or constitutional subject should reflect the lived reality of what it means to be human. An authentic representation of the legal subject is crucial to the legitimacy and effectiveness of law: to be just, the law must encompass and respond to the totality of human experience.[31]

---

[30] See Martha Albertson Fineman, 'Vulnerability and Social Justice' (2018) 53 *Valparaiso University Law Review* 341.

[31] This emphasizes the situatedness and contingency of human existence – that individuals are always already embedded in specific social, historical, and material contexts that shape their experiences and possibilities.

# TWO

# Lecture 1 – Reasoning From the Body

## Introduction to Lecture 1

This chapter explores the concept of the ontological body in order to highlight the universality of vulnerability and its implications for law and policy. It presents the foundational premise of Vulnerability Theory: as embodied beings, we are all inherently and inescapably embedded in social institutions and relationships throughout our lives. Embodied vulnerability, as well as the dependency on social institutions and relationships that it inevitably generates, presents an unambiguous challenge to (neo)liberal understandings of the nature and place of the individual. In doing so, it also demonstrates the necessity of social institutions, including those of governance.

Currently, our political theory seems precariously grounded on individualized and unrealistic notions of liberty and autonomy, reliant on a political subject fully capable of marshalling resources and able to act independently and rationally in most situations.[1] As such, these neoliberal

---

[1] Liberalism, as conceptualized by philosophers such as Thomas Hobbes and John Locke, emphasizes the protection of individual rights and the contractual nature of state responsibilities. Locke's emphasis on natural rights and government's role as protector of those rights provides a theoretical backdrop for understanding the evolution of contemporary legal frameworks in liberal democracies. Locke's ideas profoundly influenced political and constitutional debates on the appropriate balance

narratives render incomprehensible the argument that the democratic state has a primary role in defining and addressing the structural conditions necessary to achieve a communal sense of social justice. In contrast, Vulnerability Theory emphasizes the fundamental role of societal institutions in addressing dependency. Instead of working through law and policy to balance the collective, often competing interests of individuals in various situations or circumstances, the guiding premise of neoliberalism is that the state is to be restrained from interfering with economic and other social arrangements in order to protect the individual's right to liberty and choice as to what is in their best interest.[2] This preference for individual liberty and autonomy positions the individual as separate from the social or collective. It also suggests that individual wellbeing is primarily an individual responsibility.

By contrast, Vulnerability Theory recognizes that the individual is inevitably embedded within social institutions and relationships, which are not natural, but constructed entities having significance for the wellbeing of both individuals and the larger society. These institutions organize our day-to-day existence and routinely implement significant policy choices about the allocation of state (or institutional) and individual responsibility for outcomes. Vulnerability Theory thus places the realities of the body rather than the illusions of rationality and independence at the centre of inquiries into what constitutes justice. It also supports the argument that state involvement in the form of law and policy should not be seen as improper intervention into individual freedom, but a necessary

---

between individual liberty and state intervention, which are still central and influential in discussions of social justice.

[2] In the neoliberal manifestation of the ideal of guarding individual liberty, the state is mobilized in the interest of protecting the freedom of the market from governmental or regulatory policies. The market is presumed essential in providing the means and mechanisms whereby the individual is given the freedom of choice from among competing options.

(and ideally routine) mode of fulfilling state or collective responsibility in the face of individual vulnerability and dependency on legally defined institutions and relationships. Vulnerability Theory helps to formulate the questions that can help us assess the functioning of those institutions as instruments of social justice.

Beginning with the body also raises some interesting initial questions that allow us to assess the strengths and limitations of contemporary approaches to social justice issues. What do we mean when we refer to 'the body' and speculate about the legal and political significance of *embodiment*? The bodies we typically encounter in critical theory are not uniform or universal but individualized, modified, and defined by certain characteristics that give particularized bodies particular political and legal significance. Bodies are sexed, gendered, aged, raced, abled (or not), displaced, disadvantaged, and so on. The particularity of such bodies (as well as the theoretical and moral implications, it is asserted, they then seem to naturally or politically acquire) serves as the basis for legal claims against the state, as well as those perceived to be in positions of power and privilege.

The perceived social harm done to these particularized bodies (typically identified as inappropriate discrimination or exclusion from social benefits enjoyed by others) is the primary focus of most critical thought. Identification of exclusionary harm propels demands for recognition, equality, and inclusion, with an abstract ideal of equality employed to create a space of legal empowerment that allows some individuals and groups to make demands on an otherwise ideally neutral state.

As described in this first lecture, Vulnerability Theory begins with a more fundamental conception of the body: the universal ontological, anthropological conception of the body. This approach supports a different logic for analysis than that based initially on demographic differences and discrimination. It provides a basis for the reconceptualization of what constitutes harm and the necessary and appropriate remedies for that harm (see Figure 2.1 at the conclusion of this first lecture). It also highlights the necessity of considering how the body's developmental changes mean that systems of governance and the societal institutions they construct must respond and adapt in order to effectively support both individuals and society more generally.

★★★

## Lecture 1 – Reasoning From the Body

I want to begin by considering the concept of vulnerability itself. The term 'vulnerability' is widely employed. It is used in everyday discussions, as well as in academic articles and legal decisions. The meanings adopted are often shaped by an individual's disciplinary training or professional or personal experiences. Our understanding of vulnerability may also be influenced by our political, cultural, or religious perspectives. Most often, the term vulnerable has negative connotations. It designates an individual or group as weak, in need of special protection, or indicates those who are disadvantaged, discriminated against, subordinated, or oppressed.[3]

By defining specific, imposed, negative vulnerabilities, we implicitly assert vulnerability is exceptional, a characteristic of only some individuals, while others are or can become invulnerable or at least differently, less detrimentally, vulnerable than those unfortunate few. Setting up distinct categories of vulnerability in this way fragments the reality of the human condition. In doing so, it also undermines a fruitful route for articulating a comprehensive and coherent theory of state or collective responsibility.[4]

---

[3] For a discussion on the connotations of vulnerability, see Kate Brown, '"Vulnerability": Handle with Care' (2011) 5(3) *Ethics and Social Welfare* 313–21.

[4] In Vulnerability Theory, the concept of 'collective responsibility' posits that individuals are not solely responsible for their own welfare, but

When vulnerability is viewed as focused, individual, and variable, we create a conceptual dichotomy with all the practical and theoretical problems that entails. On the one hand we have a vulnerable being, inadequate or deficient, in need of protection or assistance; on the other hand stands an assumed independent, self-sufficient individual who, escaping the stigmatized designation of vulnerable, can avoid paternalistic mechanisms of state intrusion and control.[5] Importantly, what distinguishes one individual from another in this rendering is not only the claimed differences in their position as vulnerable or invulnerable. There is also a significant difference in the way these individuals are viewed in relation to others: one is dependent on others for protection or provision, the other is not.[6]

---

that society as a whole has an obligation to ensure equitable conditions and support systems. By situating individuals within a network of social relationships and institutions, Vulnerability Theory emphasizes that our wellbeing is deeply reliant on interconnected state and societal structures. Our theories of governance must address and respond to this inherent individual and inter-institutional dependence. This approach challenges the neoliberal emphasis on individual autonomy and responsibility, advocating instead for a more inclusive and responsive framework of governance and social support.

[5] This is a critical point – it references how a colloquial use of vulnerability or related concepts of differentiation and distinction as the basis for comparison among individuals can fracture the legal or political subject. In doing so, it also affects the ways in which we think of state responsibility; directed and specifically remedial, rather than routine and foundational. However, fragmented notions of vulnerability are also central to much of contemporary critical scholarship where the concepts of discrimination and inequality rely on drawing such distinctions and arguing for their rectification.

[6] In the logical progression suggested by a discrimination/equality paradigm, the designation of vulnerability serves as the assertion of harm sufficient to justify state intervention and correction. The harm is in the differentiation of circumstances. In contrast, Vulnerability Theory posits that the universality of vulnerability forms the basis for state responsibility in the form of building responsive institutional structures of resilience.

The need for assistance or protection is therefore deemed exceptional, warranted by the status of vulnerability. This dichotomy is not only inappropriate, but it also ultimately narrows and confines our vision for social justice and our aspirations for a more inclusive society.[7] The idea that some of us are not vulnerable (or that some of us are uniquely so), therefore, will operate on the individual level to disadvantage both those deemed vulnerable and those excluded from that category, as it also works on the societal level to ultimately diminish the wellbeing of the collective community.

Vulnerability Theory offers a very different understanding of vulnerability, one that can anchor a robust sense of state or collective responsibility.[8] The theory gives a specific, precise meaning to vulnerability, which differs significantly from what is commonly employed. Vulnerability is defined as a term of art used to describe a foundational concept portraying the universal human condition. Importantly, redefining vulnerability in this way is not an end in itself but merely the *initial* step (although a crucial one) in constructing an ambitious

---

Vulnerability under this approach is not an individual injury or exception but the essence of the human condition, requiring effective collective action and response. Importantly, this dichotomy affects social policies and individual perceptions by reinforcing stereotypes associated with negative views of dependency and the desirability (and achievability) of independence.

[7] Social justice is the topic of Lecture 2. In Vulnerability Theory, the idea of social justice is focused on the universal legal subject and is concerned with the organization and functioning of the social institutions and relationships that structure all of our day-to-day lives regardless of our demographic differences. These institutions (such as the family, the workplace, and the finance, education, and healthcare systems), and the relationships developed within them, constitute the very fabric of our lives, and none of us can wholly live outside of them.

[8] By redefining vulnerability as a universal human condition, Vulnerability Theory shifts the discourse from individual deficiencies to a broader socio-political context, underscoring the role of the state in mitigating vulnerability through inclusive and just policies.

project to create an alternative to current dominant ways of thinking about social justice.[9]

A reconstituted understanding of vulnerability provides us with a way to understand the nature and role of societal institutions. This institutional focus decentres the individual, concentrating our attention instead on the collective social organizations in which we live our day-to-day lives – organizations such as the family, the workplace, and the health, educational, and finance systems. These social arrangements incorporate certain norms and values reflected in the rules that bring them into existence and govern their functioning. Those rules can come from various sources other than the state. The market is one alternative source dominated by multinational corporations. Religion is another, as are industries, such as those controlling finance, pharmaceuticals, or insurance coverage. The point is that some source of power or authority will be mobilized, and rules will be imposed. The questions we should be asking are: which sources of power and what kind of rules.[10]

Vulnerability Theory advocates for the democratic state in that rule-making context, arguing that it is uniquely positioned in political and constitutional history as the legitimate

---

[9] Moving the discussion about vulnerability and its implications has proven difficult in many contexts. In many ways, the definition and use of the term are sticking points. Some scholars want to differentiate between types of vulnerability or its origins and causes – situational, layered, and so on. Others consistently use it as an alternative way of signalling disadvantage or special injury or as attached to certain phases or conditions such as childhood or disability. The idea of vulnerability as universal and its implications for ideals such as autonomy, independence, agency, and the very understanding of the individual as the centre of philosophical, political, and legal theory based on such individualistic ideals is resisted, perhaps because of its implications for the meanings of those concepts.

[10] See David Harvey, *A Brief History of Neoliberalism* (Oxford University Press 2005), which provides a comprehensive examination of neoliberalism's rise, emphasizing the increasing inequality and erosion of social welfare.

mechanism for constructing the rules necessary for a just and inclusive society.[11] Let me emphasize, this is *not* an argument that the state functions in that way currently, merely that it has more *potential* for doing so than do the alternatives. This potential has been impaired and frustrated by impoverished, simplistic notions of individual equality and liberty, which tolerate only a limited, constrained vision of the state.[12] The resulting diminished notions of state responsibility have left the hapless individual condemned to manoeuvre within a system of unrepresentative and unregulated societal institutions. Vulnerability Theory challenges this impaired vision, arguing the necessity of crafting a regime of social or inclusive justice built around an ethics of care or collective responsibility.[13] This point brings me, of course, to the topic for discussion today: the theoretical necessity of reasoning from the body.[14]

---

[11] Vulnerability Theory accepts the inevitability of state action and the reality of law, arguing that the state is always at least a residual actor in the creation and maintenance of social arrangements. The theory advocates that the state, however it defines its mandate, must be responsive to the realities of human vulnerability and attentive to the institutional structures necessary to address that vulnerability. This idea of the appropriately responsive state is developed more fully in subsequent lectures.

[12] The impoverished visions of state responsibility are apparent in the simplistic senses of individual responsibility and self-sufficiency, which complements a corresponding notion of individual liberty, as well as the unrealistic abstract ideals it valorizes, such as autonomy and independence.

[13] While the concept of care is found in feminist literature beginning in the 1980s, I use it here in an expanded sense, moving well beyond the needs associated with the family or ideas of individual dependence and necessity of caretaking. Vulnerability Theory argues for the development of an ethic of governmental responsibility (or care) built on recognition and acceptance of universal and constant vulnerability. Vulnerability and its implications are inherent to the human condition and the necessity to respond to them forms the basis for the legitimacy of governance in the first place. (See Lecture 3 (Chapter 4).)

[14] This initial point forms what might be called a 'first principle', or foundational assertion of Vulnerability Theory. It is the material or empirical reality upon which later concepts and assertions rely. The basic

## 2.1 The body

The body in Vulnerability Theory is understood as a universal, ontological concept.[15] All human beings are *embodied* beings. Stating this obvious truth does not mean ignoring the differences among bodies. However, when and how those differences matter on a theoretical level requires exploration beyond merely asserting their existence.

At this point, I want to highlight an important aspect of vulnerability analysis. There are two related components in the analysis. First, we are fundamentally embodied beings, therefore, we should begin with the body. Second, because of the attributes and limitations of those bodies, we are inescapably *embedded* in social institutions and relationships.[16] With this component, we address the social implications of the body: what embodiment inherently means in political, economic, and other institutional terms. Vulnerability Theory

---

logic of a vulnerability argument is built on this foundational premise, which stands in stark contrast to the image imposed by liberal legal principles, which typically incorporates abstract notions of rationality and individuality at its core.

[15] In emphasizing the universal, ontological status of the body, Vulnerability Theory contests the prevalent legal and political abstractions that often overlook or underestimate the physical basis of human existence. This perspective is crucial as it lays the groundwork for understanding how societal structures must adapt to the inherent physical realities of human life, rather than idealized notions of independence and autonomy. This perspective calls for a shift towards policies that acknowledge our inherent physical and social vulnerability and the need for a responsive state.

[16] Recognizing that human beings are of necessity social beings and that the realities of our bodies mean we cannot avoid being dependent on institutional structures is a fundamental contribution of Vulnerability Theory. This reliance or dependence on social relationships challenges the notion of the liberal individual as an autonomous, self-sufficient entity and should mandate rethinking, as well as a corresponding repositioning of legal and social policies so as to cast them as more inclusive and responsive to the human condition.

ultimately focuses on the justice and effects of such social relationships and institutions.

At this point, I want to acknowledge that we know that some social relationships and institutions historically have been formed around demographic differences such as race, sex, and ability in ways that are now recognized as exploitative, undemocratic, and oppressive.[17] The specific harms resulting from targeted exclusion and marginalization certainly justify legal responses. Individual or group damages may be warranted, as may affirmative action, emergency relief, or injunctions. However, the desire to remedy harm to a specific group should not eclipse the search for a vision of state or collective responsibility that reaches beyond discrimination and disaster. In other words, it is also important to develop a universal social-justice project that, while it incorporates specific oppressions and marginalization, reaches beyond to consider injury or harm conceived as universal, collective, and structural.

The concern here is redefining the baseline, reimagining the foundation or floor for defining state responsibility, and asserting social justice. Existing anti-discrimination jurisprudence implicitly incorporates and reinforces, rather than challenges, the existing baseline: the logic of discrimination is that certain actions are a deviation or departure from a norm that is presumed in and of itself to be acceptable, even desirable. Discrimination or exclusion and marginalization are then cast

---

[17] I find it necessary to emphasize this point early in a vulnerability analysis, since there is a tendency on the part of some who are deeply committed to identity-based analysis and anti-discrimination methodology to interpret anything that presumes to be universal as ignoring, erasing, or minimizing the historic harms justified on the basis of certain demographic identities. A vulnerability analysis does not deny such harm or the need for remedy directed to compensate it. It simply argues that identity-based harm, in many instances, does not perceive the full extent, nature, or origin of a governmental failure. Nor does it adequately support the type of comprehensive and institutional (not group) remedy that would be required in order to adequately address the issues.

as the harms that the remedies of inclusion and equal treatment can resolve. Vulnerability Theory, by contrast, asserts that this current baseline or foundation may in and of itself be defective and unjust because it fails to reflect the realities of the universal human condition.

Vulnerability Theory further argues that, to reflect those realities, it is essential that we reason from the body – the body is understood as an ontological or anthropological universalized concept. The body is understood as a fundamental material reality, that inevitably changes over time since it is developmental in nature.[18] Regardless of constructed demographic categories, the physical body will inevitably change, and those changes will affect both the physical and social needs, wellbeing, and stability of the individual.[19] In addition, the reality of such

---

[18] Highlighting differences by focusing on the developmental nature of the body, rather than drawing on demographic differences, is theoretically important. The developmental aspects of the human condition are often either ignored or overlooked (particularly in the use of concepts assuming equality, such as agency, contract, and consent) or compartmentalized (as is done by designating children or some elderly and disabled individuals as incomplete or lesser subjects in contrast to the idealized adult fully functioning and independent subject) in political and legal theory. In the lecture, I used a PowerPoint slide of the developmental stages of life from infancy to old age. The slide, in visualizing the inevitable changes over time in the human body, grounds the important idea that, to be truly responsive to the realities of the vulnerable subject, state responsibility must extend over the life course, rather than being confined to only one stage of life.

[19] This point underscores what a vulnerability perspective casts as one of the major failings of the liberal legal approach. The liberal reliance on rationality, choice, agency, and so on to craft a restrained state in service to individual liberty and autonomy means that state responsibility applies only to some individuals at any one time and only at some stages of development for all individuals. Liberal theory routinely exempts groups from full subjectivity – this was true of women (and slaves, servants, and even non-property holders) historically and remains true of children and many disabled or elderly individuals not deemed sufficiently independent. Vulnerability Theory would extend responsibility for individual wellbeing

individual changes over the life course will have significant implications for society.

Note that, in considering the inevitability of bodily change, on the individual level, change can be positive as well as negative. The ontological body is not only, or not even primarily, the site of decline. It is not merely weak and fragile. Its developmental changes are also the occasion for innovation, creativity, and the expansion of opportunity and capacity.[20]

## 2.2 Liberty and independence – ignoring the body

Significantly, on a public policy level, some positive changes can be encouraged, or negative changes deterred, and many changes are, in fact, predictable. But the unavoidable fact about the body as an ontological entity is that profound changes are inescapable, and many are not within our control; some may not even be predictable. This susceptibility to change defines the human condition in vulnerability terms.

Of course, all these facts about the body and developmental change are perfectly obvious. A fair question might be why I dwell on developmental changes in this presentation. I do so because the societal and policy implications of this developmental aspect of the ontological body are resisted or ignored both by individuals and by governments. Our embodied vulnerability is not in the foundation for the laws, norms, values, and aspirations we have established for our societies and their institutions. It is not the bedrock of our understanding of responsibility, in either its individual or collective dimension.

Instead, our laws and politics glorify abstract notions of equality, freedom, and autonomy as though these were desirable

---

across the entire life course – although that responsibility might be met by the creation and monitoring of mediating institutions, such as the family.

[20] For an analysis of the positive aspects of bodily changes, see Chris Shilling, *The Body and Social Theory* (SAGE Publications 2012).

and attainable human qualities. An idealized legal subject is cast as independent, autonomous, and liberty-seeking, leaving the body behind. This oversimplified perspective I refer to as the 'Brooks Brothers' version of the legal subject.[21] As a result, law and policy only very narrowly define the interests and legitimate province of the state as well as the extent of state or collective responsibility for both individual and societal wellbeing. And law is not alone in this failure to neglect the body. Other disciplines also disregard the vulnerable subject in spinning out their theories.

The liberty-seeking reasonable man trope found in law and politics also manifests as the 'rational actor' in economics, the 'autonomous consenting being' in ethics, and the 'competent rights holder' who is capable of pursuing and protecting interests across various domains. He informs the doctor/patient relationship, is present throughout accounts of history, psychology, political science, sociology, and so on. These underdeveloped, incomplete subjects of theory are taken out of the social relationships and institutions, which are the very structures in which we both experience vulnerability and depend on the resources to ameliorate it. These theoretical subjects are radically individualized subjects, abandoned to conceptual devices such as consent, contract, agency, and rights, which are woefully inadequate to address the inescapable

---

[21] Brooks Brothers is a clothing brand, recognized as one of the oldest clothiers in the US. The brand became synonymous with Ivy League and preppy style, offering conservative clothing often associated with American business attire and traditional values. At this point in the lecture, I showed a slide of a group of seemingly trim, white-male business suit-clad individuals purposefully striding forward in a line. This meme embodies a parody of independence and autonomy (even as it does so with an excess of conformity), which can be contrasted with subsequent images of individuals in relationship to each other, depicting vulnerability and dependence and our inevitable reliance on social structures and relationships that actually form the realities of our day-to-day lives.

and lifelong dependence on society and its institutions that our vulnerability entails.

Of course, in a world in which vulnerability is resisted and autonomy and independence define the legal subject, as well as limiting the aspirations for the institutions of our mundane existence, individuals are bound to fail. And we see that individual failure around us today in the neoliberal dystopia created by and through the operation of law and policies. The abdication of state responsibility has resulted in distinctive social harms: poverty, deprivation, and inequality for many in society. These are individual harms produced by the profound neglect or callous indifference and disregard on the part of the state to the realities of the human condition. But the harm extends beyond that done to the individual. Such profound neglect is a violation of the very rationale for the existence of the government and law,[22] a rejection of the responsibility and principles that legitimate the constitution of the state in the first instance. They should be understood, therefore, as *constitutional* harms.

## 2.3 Dependence and the embedded vulnerable subject[23]

This brings us to the embedded component of the theory and the concept of dependency. The fundamental reality is that the physical and developmental realities of the human body render us inescapably embedded in and dependent upon social relations and institutions throughout life. Dependency is not a

---

[22] I return to his point of constitutional harm in the lecture on injury by redefining what should be considered a 'constitutional injury' to include not only harmful or inappropriate state intervention but more significantly (and commonly) state neglect, inattention, and failure to respond or be responsive to the implications of vulnerability and dependency, which constitutes in Vulnerability Theory the very failure of the legitimating purpose of government.

[23] See Figure 2.1.

variation or example of vulnerability but the manifestation or realization of it.[24] Unfortunately, we resist this realization both as individuals and as politicians and policymakers. Importantly, dependency also should not be conceived only, or primarily, in negative terms either, just like vulnerability. It is profoundly generative.[25]

Our innate dependency is the impetus for us as a species to come together in families and communities to form political organizations, both local and international. Our dependency is the very basis for society and its institutions. Social relationships and structures are necessary to provide the resources that simultaneously give us the ability to adapt, adjust, survive, and even thrive, given our vulnerability. In Vulnerability Theory, we call these accumulated resources 'resilience'. Importantly, no one is born resilient. Rather, resilience is acquired over time within social institutions and relationships – institutions and relationships that are created by and through law and policy.

Note that, on an individual level, dependence on social institutions, although constant throughout life, varies and fluctuates over time in response to the circumstances or developmental stage in which the individual is located.[26]

---

[24] In other words, while vulnerability is an inherent characteristic of the human condition, dependency is the expression of this vulnerability in social and institutional contexts.

[25] Generative is used here in the sense that dependency is productive of social relationships – 'initiating, relating to or capable of production or reproduction', as per *Oxford English Dictionary*, www.oed.com/diction ary/generative_adj.

[26] To some extent, I am contrasting dependency with vulnerability. Vulnerability is both constant and universal while dependency, although it is also universal, is variable or episodic. Dependency can be thought of as the periodic or expected realization or implication of our vulnerability – the difference between manifestation or realization and prospect or potential. Dependency is linked to the body but focuses us on our inevitable reliance on social institutions or the 'embedded' aspect of the theory.

For example, in infancy we are inevitably dependent on care from social institutions such as the family. But the birth family recedes, and other institutions typically become more prominent later in an individual's life when the need for care arises only occasionally, such as when we are ill or injured. In other words, individual dependence on any specific institutional arrangement can be thought of as episodic, alterable, and circumstantial.

However, it is important to recognize and theoretically address the reality that dependency on some set of social institutions and relationships – be they the market, financial, and employment systems or educational and healthcare institutions – is inevitable and ongoing for everyone throughout life. The family and the educational systems will shape an individual's success or failure in later encounters with the employment system or within the political and civic/social systems, all of which will have implications for the ability of the individual to form and maintain a family, as well as ensure their wellbeing in retirement and old age. Individual dependency on social institutions and relationships, therefore, cannot be perceived as deviant or exceptional; it is the norm, inevitable, and it is inherent in the human condition.

I want to mention another important dimension of dependency. And this is the institutional component that goes beyond the individual component. And here I want to introduce the concept of 'derivative dependency'. To explain this, let us go back to the family. Within the family, those who are assigned the social identity of caretaker are what I call derivatively dependent. They depend on resources to successfully accomplish their social role, which is to care for the developmentally dependent individual who is exemplified, of course, by the child. Sometimes those resources come from within the family – a spouse or partner, a grandparent – but they also must come from other social institutions.

In other words, the family alone is not sufficient for the task of handling dependency. Its success is linked to the successful functioning of other social institutions, including the educational and healthcare systems and the employment system or market institutions, more generally, as well as the social welfare system. This institutional interdependency is not only true of the family. That is to say, the family is not the only dependent institution. Rather, it is the norm. It is true of all social institutions. So, we begin to see how these institutions are inevitably, undeniably symbiotically linked and, together, they function to reproduce society, providing for individual and societal wellbeing.

## 2.4 Conclusion – institutions and interdependence[27]

Vulnerability Theory mandates that the individual always be placed within complex institutional contexts in thinking about how we should assess state responsibility and how we should judge our politics.[28] Therefore, from a Vulnerability Theory perspective (reasoning from the body and recognizing dependency), there are two significant points of focus, and both are currently sites where the state has failed in fulfilling its responsibility. First, consider the design and allocation of authority across societal institutions. These social institutions and relationships upon which we depend are ultimately the products of law and policy. Even if the state is not visibly and actively engaged in defining these institutions and their roles within society, its past engagement (such as deeming some functions or institutions of primarily private rather than public

---

[27] See Figure 2.2.

[28] This is why concepts such as autonomy and independence are not primary in a vulnerability analysis. The individual is inherently dependent on social institutions and structures, even in adulthood, and cannot be adequately understood independent of an appreciation for how they function in the reproduction of both the individual and the society in which we must inevitably live our day-to-day lives.

concern) affects the present arrangements.[29] So, the history of defining these institutions is worth exploring and critiquing. And when the state has decided not to be actively present in an institutional arrangement, it will be fruitful to inquire what or who fills in in the absence of the state. Who or what is making the rules, and what are those rules? Who or what is left out, and who or what is privileged or disadvantaged?

These societal institutions serve essential roles in the reproduction of society and, of course, are crucial to the wellbeing of individuals. They confer recognition and structure accommodation. They supply the often-essential arrangements for future generations, as well as those already in existence. So, we must ask – how effectively do they provide individual resilience and/or the societal benefits used to justify their existence politically? As already noted, the interinstitutional relationships represented here are complex. The family, the workplace, the financial system, and so on are symbiotic parts of a larger whole. The particular proportions, collaborations, and limitations of these interinstitutional relationships are not accidental, natural, or inevitable but the product of political and policy choices.

A second point of focus and critique for Vulnerability Theory is intra-institutional. Here, we look at the individual social identities created within each institution. These social (or institutional) identities correspond to the social functions of the institutions in which they are located, but they also define the roles that individuals are to assume within these institutions. These social identities are paired, complementary, and often of necessity unequal relationships – parent/child, employer/employee, shareholder/consumer, doctor/patient, lender/borrower, and

---

[29] This is the core idea behind the concept of the responsive state: since law (rules which legitimate coercive power) are necessary to the effective operation of social institutions and relationships, either directly or in establishing the background conditions for 'private' exercises of authority, state responsibility, while it can be delegated, can never be totally abandoned.

so on.[30] These institutional identities are also legal identities in which individual responsibility is distributed using the mundane everyday law such as contract, corporation, employment, family, criminal, tort law, and so on. If they cannot be and should not be equal, how do we determine if and when they are just? Who should be privileged in these relationships, how, and why? How do we construct relationships of asymmetrical responsibility?

Vulnerability Theory explores both the institutional and the individual relationships of distribution, placing the vulnerable subject and dependency at the centre of law and policy, displacing the autonomous, independent liberal subject that now dominates theory. In doing so, Vulnerability Theory poses important questions about how we understand justice and responsibility and also provides a critique of the status quo as well as a way to imagine a better, more just future. Vulnerability Theory's inherent adaptability ensures it will continue to address new and emerging forms of challenge and opportunity, keeping our legal and policy frameworks dynamic and responsive to the evolving needs of society.

---

[30] The idea that many, if not most, social relationships defined within these institutional contexts are inherently unequal is a significant critique Vulnerability Theory offers of liberal legal and political approaches. Liberal legal theory has papered over this inequality by manipulation of the legal subject (excluding some from full legal subjectivity, such as children) or through the creation of legal fictions (most notably the idea of 'contract', as in social contract or employment contract, or 'informed consent', which facilitates situations like doctor/patient agreements to treat, but also through the notion that parental rights are based on the premise that parents routinely act in the 'best interests' of their children). Although, in many instances, these fictions may bear some relation to the realities of the situation, applied unreflectively, they allow those theorists to avoid the difficult question of the degree of ongoing responsibility the state has in establishing and monitoring inherently unequal social or institutional relationships that should generate rules of unequal or asymmetric responsibility to function justly. Lecture 4 addresses inevitable inequality more fully.

Figure 2.1 organizes the two pillars of Vulnerability Theory, which together constitute the human condition: we are both Embodied and Embedded beings. Embodied vulnerability refers to the inherent and inevitable aspects of the human condition, while Embedded vulnerability addresses the societal structures and positions that can exacerbate or mitigate individual vulnerabilities. Placing these concepts side by side allows us to compare and contrast the line of reasoning that proceeds from each.

Reading down each vertical listing, we can see the progression of analysis as to who or what is the focus of analysis, what is considered to constitute harm, what is deemed the necessary response to that harm, which laws are to be applied, and the values and logic expressed in those laws.

A vulnerability approach argues that, in order to achieve a truly inclusive and comprehensive sense of social justice, we must focus on and understand the systemic or structural, as well as resolving how to effectively address the individual or particular.

Figure 2.2 sets out the distributional aspect of a vulnerability analysis. Note that more than economic benefits or burdens are distributed through state law and policy. Equally important are the structural, ideological, and cultural benefits that facilitate and accommodate day-to-day essential activities, such as assigning value or legitimating position and practice.

The first level of distribution shows the symbiotic relationship and dependence of institutional structures on each other and within the entirety of society. The second level pictures the distribution of responsibility within each institution according to the social or institutional identities formed within the institution. These are the relationships of inherent inequality that are currently easy to ignore in liberal theory, with its focus on the individual rather than the relational and its adherence to values such as rationality, consent, and independence.

Figure 2.1: Comparing the embodied and embedded pillars of Vulnerability Theory

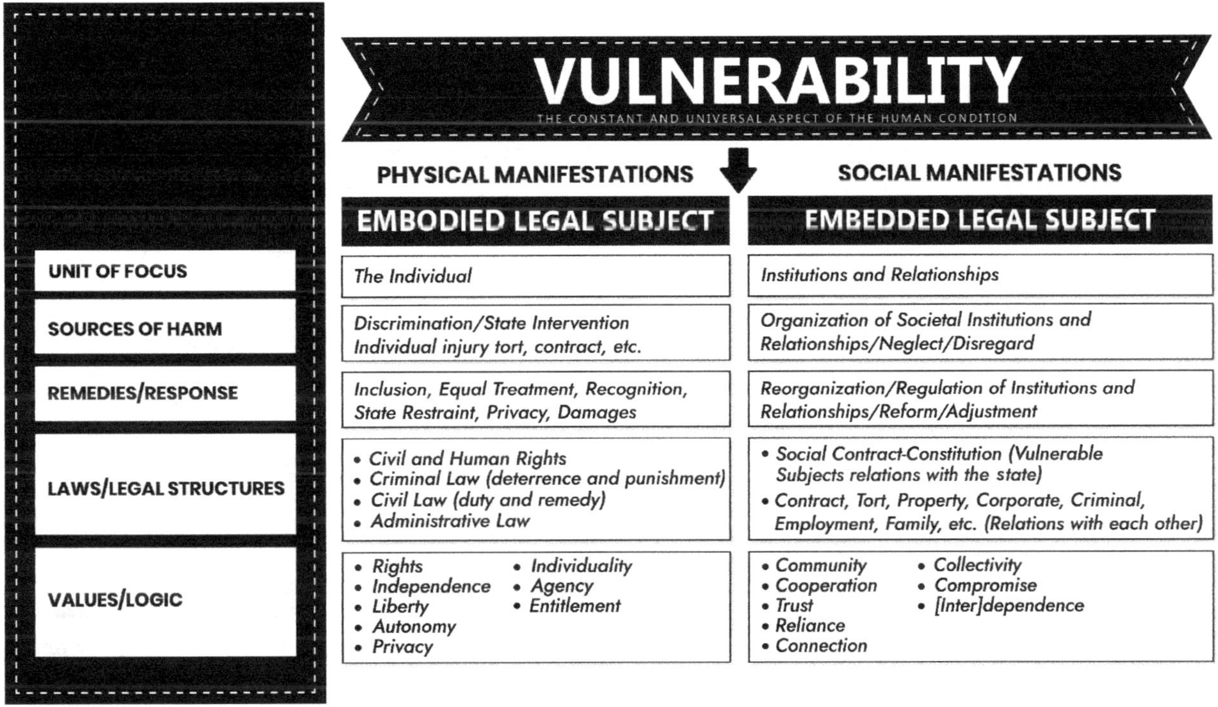

## VULNERABILITY
THE CONSTANT AND UNIVERSAL ASPECT OF THE HUMAN CONDITION

| | PHYSICAL MANIFESTATIONS | SOCIAL MANIFESTATIONS |
|---|---|---|
| | **EMBODIED LEGAL SUBJECT** | **EMBEDDED LEGAL SUBJECT** |
| **UNIT OF FOCUS** | The Individual | Institutions and Relationships |
| **SOURCES OF HARM** | Discrimination/State Intervention Individual injury tort, contract, etc. | Organization of Societal Institutions and Relationships/Neglect/Disregard |
| **REMEDIES/RESPONSE** | Inclusion, Equal Treatment, Recognition, State Restraint, Privacy, Damages | Reorganization/Regulation of Institutions and Relationships/Reform/Adjustment |
| **LAWS/LEGAL STRUCTURES** | • Civil and Human Rights<br>• Criminal Law (deterrence and punishment)<br>• Civil Law (duty and remedy)<br>• Administrative Law | • Social Contract-Constitution (Vulnerable Subjects relations with the state)<br>• Contract, Tort, Property, Corporate, Criminal, Employment, Family, etc. (Relations with each other) |
| **VALUES/LOGIC** | • Rights    • Individuality<br>• Independence    • Agency<br>• Liberty    • Entitlement<br>• Autonomy<br>• Privacy | • Community    • Collectivity<br>• Cooperation    • Compromise<br>• Trust    • [Inter]dependence<br>• Reliance<br>• Connection |

Figure 2.2: Institutions and interdependence

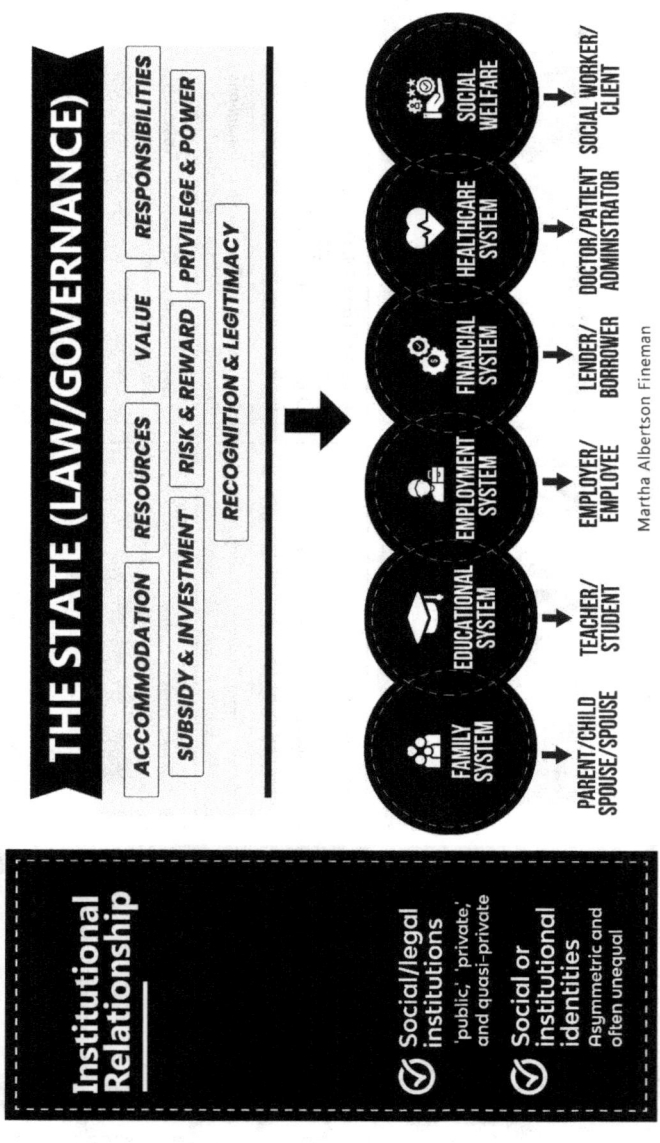

# THREE

# Lecture 2 – Social Justice

## Introduction to Lecture 2

This lecture considers the difficulty of conceiving a truly collective approach to individual and societal wellbeing in the context of currently dominant ways of thinking about social justice. Certainly, a great deal of resistance is formed in the shadow of the individualistic non-interventionist rhetoric that dominates contemporary political discourse on the conservative level. However, the difficulty in accepting a truly all-encompassing notion of justice – one that has more universal roots – is also found in a liberal rights-based, anti-discrimination sense of social justice. This approach focuses on the compelling need to respond to the legacies of historic injustices that affirmatively targeted generally ignored, or inequitably impacted, specific groups within society, and is decidedly different than that presented by the non-interventionists.

The dominant frame for progressive critics of governmental policies, rights-based anti-discrimination approaches echo an undeniable reality. The challenge, therefore, for those seeking a broader, more generally inclusive, notion of social justice, is to imagine an overall theoretical approach that can encompass and advance remedies for past failures and faults evidenced by discriminatory policies and practices while also serving as a foundational, universally applicable, and coherent theory arguing for the just treatment of all in society going forward.

This ambition to create an expansive notion of social justice seems particularly crucial. Today we inhabit a world of dynamic complexity, insecurity, and uncertainty unimaginable to the political actors who shaped foundational governing documents, such as the US Constitution during the eighteenth century. These documents were based on both egalitarian and liberty-oriented principles that valorized the individual and minimized the need for governmental action (interference).

Considering the nature of the collective crises we confront today, one might well wonder whether the principles defining the aspirations of those living under very different circumstances can adequately or effectively address contemporary concerns. What is required in many situations is *not* restraint and non-intervention, but responsiveness and involvement on the part of the state. A United Nations report on social justice[1] highlighted how modern politics used liberal principles to shift focus from collective good to individual rights, complicating efforts for a broadly conceived social justice framework.

In a vulnerability analysis, the question of policy is not primarily framed in terms of whether there is a 'right' belonging to the individual but whether this a 'responsibility' placed upon the state. The basic premise is that, given human vulnerability, there is an unavoidable governmental or law-making responsibility to form and monitor legal institutions responsive to that vulnerability – a governmental duty to care about, and be responsive to, the realities of the human condition.

A vulnerability analysis explores whether and how this duty has been expressed in the creation and design of legal institutions and relationships within any given society. The idea of resilience is relevant in this context. Produced within social institutions over time, resilience is crucial in understanding

---

[1] United Nations Department of Economic and Social Affairs, Division for Social Policy and Development, *Social Justice in an Open World: The Role of the United Nations*, UN Doc. ST/ESA/305 (2006), https://www.un.org/esa/socdev/documents/ifsd/SocialJustice.pdf, accessed September 26, 2024.

how state responsibility must be manifested, broadening our inquiry of what constitutes justice to encompass more than the issues typically included in a discussion of *individual* rights. It brings into focus the complexities and symbiotic nature of the institutional arrangements in which the individual is inevitably located and the social structural aspects of a justice assessment.

As a result, a social justice approach would consider institutional contexts, being attentive to the complementary and intersecting structural arrangements, to imagine the possibility of constructing a comprehensive and coordinated system of social justice, one that would serve as a foundation for society by asking how we can and should structure various institutional arrangements to respond effectively to the complex, lived realities of the human condition.

Resilience allows individuals to survive and thrive, highlighting the importance of just and effective institutional arrangements. The last three lectures all address this challenge: Lecture 2 considers what an inclusive social justice scheme might entail; Lecture 3 reconceives our notions of what constitutes injury; and Lecture 4 focuses on the inherent inequality of fundamental social relationships and the need for an idea of justice that incorporates the governmental obligation to monitor and mitigate the resulting asymmetric power relationships.

★★★

## Lecture 2 – Social Justice

In the first lecture, we discussed reasoning from the body or the importance of beginning with the body as an ontological or anthropological material reality in building theory. Therefore, I want to begin here by reflecting on what vulnerability is *not* in the context of understanding the implications of Vulnerability Theory on our ideas about social justice.[2] Vulnerability is not

---

[2] I wrote a short declaration titled 'What Vulnerability Theory Is and Is Not' in frustration after a workshop during the fourth year after

simply a substitute for dependency on care. Nor is its theoretical potential captured by concepts such as weakness, fragility, precariousness, or being at risk.[3]

As an initial starting point, it is vital to recognize that there is no position of invulnerability. As embodied beings, we are all vulnerable.[4] In addition, from a legal perspective, vulnerability

> beginning the Vulnerability and the Human Condition Initiative. So many of the sessions got bogged down in discussions about the 'real' or 'best' meaning of vulnerability and never moved to what I considered the more significant questions of the appropriate allocation of responsibility for the basic institutions of everyday life. I have come to realize that this definition fixation was perhaps an unavoidable consequence of using a word that was not only typically found in debates in a variety of areas, but also highly stigmatized. I had encountered the same sort of resistance to an attempt to rehabilitate a stigmatized term in my earlier work on dependency. In that context, I argued that there simply was not another word capable of expressing the meaning and significance of the condition I wanted to explore. Rather than my having to find a different term, it was necessary to explore the implications of an altered, more reality-reflecting understanding of dependency. The same need for us to revisit and reconsider our uses of the concept of vulnerability. The problem is not with the word vulnerability, but in our understanding of the range and depth of what it expresses about the human condition. Further, by our failure to understand vulnerability means we do not clearly see its implications for our own lives and the need for reconsideration of certain political and ethical judgments. See Martha Albertson Fineman, 'What Vulnerability Theory Is and Is Not' (2021) *Vulnerability and the Human Condition Initiative*, https://scholarblogs.emory.edu/vulnerability/2021/02/01/is-and-is-not/.

[3] As I explain later (and several times) the reality and potentiality of vulnerability are not captured (even though it is often wrongly contained) by casting it in negative terms.

[4] I would assert that on some level many of us know, both empirically and intuitively from the context of our own lives, that there is no position of invulnerability (no matter how much we might wish that were not so), but do not have the conceptual tools to place that experiential realization within a theoretical (and therefore distant and objective) framework. This seems to be one of the most difficult basic concepts for people (particularly in the US) to grasp. They consistently want to dislodge vulnerability from the theory's assertion that it defines the core or essence of the human

is not just another way of talking about discrimination or signalling disadvantage. Vulnerability is not merely one among many possible identities adopted in arguing for equality and civil and political rights. Nor is vulnerability situational, although certain circumstances or social situations may reveal vulnerability in ways that make its existence harder to ignore than others.

So, we recognize that childhood is a stage in which our shared vulnerability is most evident – when we command the fewest resources and therefore have the least resilience.[5] But it is theoretically important to understand childhood as a universally experienced stage in the human condition, not a distinct identity. As a consequence, it is important not to position children as a uniquely vulnerable subgroup of beings, a 'vulnerable population'. To reinforce this, we might refer not to the child but to 'the vulnerable subject in childhood', recognizing that it is a stage that has particular challenges and implications for the development and wellbeing of the universal vulnerable subject.[6]

---

condition to make it describe a mere finite situation or circumstance – to make it episodic or temporary, accidental, and avoidable, rather than fundamental and inescapable.

[5] Resilience is explained in more depth later in this lecture. The concept refers to assets or resources we accumulate through social institutions and relationships throughout our lives. These assets may be material (such as economic or concrete items, social or relational (such as family connections and a sense of belonging to a group or cause), ecological (such as those found in the position we find ourselves within both the natural and constructed environment), and existential (such as the strength or security we gather from belief and commitment to ideas or expressions of the meaning and purpose of our actions). Importantly, resilience is not something we are born with, but is accumulated (and expended) within social institutions and relationships throughout the life course.

[6] Using the developmental stage of childhood to create a distinct legal identity (vulnerable children) is common in legal policy and doctrine. Vulnerability Theory by contrast, recognizes that the universal and constant vulnerability of our being is more evident in childhood, but

It is extremely important to remember, in discussing the meaning of vulnerability, however, that we only *begin* with the body. It is essential to move from that empirical reality to expand the theoretical frame: moving beyond an understanding of the ontological body as the initial site of our universal vulnerability, to consider the implications of that realization. This consideration of implications constitutes the embedded or institutional dimensions of Vulnerability Theory – as embodied beings, we are, throughout life, dependent on social institutions and relationships that form the infrastructure for our day-to-day lives.[7]

## 3.1 Defining social justice

Considering this structural or institutional dimension brings me to the topic for this lecture – social justice. The article I suggested as background reading for today's lecture[8] begins

---

attributes this to the fact that this is the stage of life when, typically and not unexpectedly, we have not accumulated the resources or resilience we will need to manage or mediate our vulnerability. Childhood is a universal stage in human development. Using terms such as vulnerable children in Vulnerability Theory would be the same as saying 'human humans'. On a related (and equally important) level, childhood is the stage in life when the vulnerable subject is most obviously and visibly dependent on social institutions and relationships for our very survival. To bring these two points together: perhaps the way to express the concern we have for the vulnerable child is to instead talk about the child who does not have the access to the resources and structures we all depend upon for survival, and which are generated and maintained by society and the social institutions and relationships it constructs using law and policy.

[7] The institutional aspects of the theory are set out in diagram form in Figure 2.2 in Chapter 2. These institutions are the creatures of law and structure family, work, health, wealth, transactions, and consequences that make up our everyday existence. The institutions are symbolically related and also determine the relational dynamics and obligations of the social relationships within them (such as employer/employee, parent/child, landlord/tenant, and so on).

[8] 'Vulnerability and Social Justice' (2019) 53 *Valparaiso Law Review* 341.

with the question: 'What, if anything, does the designation of "social" add to the ideal of justice?' I asked what exactly does the term 'social' mean, and how do we achieve it? Certainly, social justice is a key phrase, in use in many progressive circles, forming the conceptual basis for programmes, conferences, and publications.

After raising this question (and in the best law and society scholarly tradition) I did a bit of 'empirical research', asking other scholars how they defined social justice. Several people indicated they had never even considered the definitional question. When people did respond, interestingly there was no consensus. For some, social justice was just another way of talking about individual human rights, such as the assurance of equality and lack of discrimination (particularly focused on gender justice, racial justice, and so on). For others, there was a more social dimension to justice, although it also tended to be organized around a particular group rather than formed in general societal terms (like 'environmental justice' framed as disparate impact on racial minorities). For a few, social justice seemed to be no more than a conclusion or judgment that was applied to a particular situation or circumstance – people knew social justice when they saw it (and, presumably, when they did not).

In thinking about the potential theoretical contrast between the *individual* and the *social* (or the 'particular' and the 'collective'), I also resorted to dictionary definitions,[9] as well as unearthing other conventional sources. In that way, I found 'Social Justice in an Open World', a 2006 publication by the UN Department of Economic and Social Affairs.[10] This report

---

[9] This was not a particularly helpful strategy, the dictionary definition typically merely referring to the communal as contrasted with the individual aspects of society.

[10] United Nations Department of Economic and Social Affairs, Division for Social Policy and Development, *Social Justice in an Open World: The Role of the United Nations*, UN Doc. ST/ESA/305 (2006), https://desapublicati ons.un.org/publications/social-justice-open-world-role-united-nations.

was particularly significant in developing my own thoughts about social justice.

The report initially indicated that 'unlike justice in the broad sense, social justice is a relatively recent concept', which helpfully placed the concept in its historical context. The report further indicated that the term *social* justice originally was associated with the 'struggles surrounding the industrial revolution and the advent of socialist (or social democratic and Christian democratic) views on the proper organization of society'. Social justice was used as a rallying cry for progressive activists and was broadly understood as ensuring 'the fair and compassionate distribution of the fruits of economic growth'. This involved not only the distribution of wealth but also public benefits. It was anticipated that social justice would be accomplished by giving the authority to pursue something called the 'common good' to *public* institutions.[11]

This historic understanding of social justice is certainly consistent with a contemporary Vulnerability Theory perspective on responsibility. However, looking beyond the historic origins of the term, the report expressed pessimism when it came to the question of whether the idea of social justice could be effective in pursuing the common good' in any meaningful way today.[12] Of particular interest from a vulnerability perspective, the report indicated that contemporary politics, emphasizing *individual* equality and liberty, had complicated the notion of a *public* project undertaken for something termed the common or *public* good.

---

[11] This is an important modifier – 'public' institutions were specified in contrast to the 'private' market and its institutions.

[12] Perhaps part of this negative reaction to the social was the then contemporary association of governmental action undertaken for the collective good with socialism or communism.

## 3.2 Centring the individual in conceptions of justice

The UN report explained that, over time, the term 'social justice' has lost much of its social focus. Its definition was reshaped by emerging political, economic, and cultural forces, noting that perhaps the most effective force working against a collectively focused sense of social justice was a robust commitment to individualism.[13] Justice had come to be seen as best achieved through the promotion of the individual and the formulation of individual rights. In this context, the idea of collective responsibility or advocacy of state action to promote something called the public good might be considered inherently suspect, if not heartily condemned.

Individualized notions of equality and liberty are often construed as protection from illegitimate intrusions on narrowly defined notions of personal choice, agency, and autonomy, which tends to confound the very idea of state action to affect something called social or collective justice. And what is 'good' is not seen as legitimately determined through the exercise of collective authority, but by the whim of the individual.

There are two dominant strains of individualism relevant in the UN report. One, of course, is progressive: an equality-focused, individual rights agenda.[14] And the second is

---

[13] The concept of the individual has also evolved in critical discourse. The individual in critical theory is typically not the genetic individual, but either a member of a demographically defined group or a group historically oppressed or persecuted. It is that group-identified individuality that lays claim to violate the libertarian individual's right to be left alone.

[14] The liberal (or libertarian) conception of individualism expressed in the UN report is also consistent with some forms of collectively conceived arguments for justice. For example, anti-discrimination approaches are individualized in that the group-defined category that is the basis for discrimination prevents the individual from being judged on his or her own merits – it is a distortion of the individualized meritocracy deemed to otherwise prevail. Neoliberal free-market ideology also asserts individual

neoliberalism, which is market-based and in which state authority and power are mobilized to protect the market in the so-called interest of the individual and society. Neoliberalism is certainly typically considered to be on a very different pole of the political spectrum than an individual rights analysis. However, both tend to adhere to an individual-focused, rather than a collectivized conception of justice.[15]

The report also suggests that, over the course of the twentieth century, justice has increasingly become understood in economic terms.[16] Across the political spectrum, politicians generally agree that a society has a fundamental responsibility to equalize and facilitate opportunities for individuals to engage in productive economic activities of their own choice. In addition, although there are areas of dispute about preconditions, there is a consensus that economic and social rewards are justly distributed when that distribution is the product of individual talent, initiative, and effort. Governmental action is legitimate when it provides freedom and options for the individual – the 'freedom to consume', as well as the freedom 'to determine what one does with one's life to maximize economic potential and social position as one defines it'.

This political consensus is rooted in economic opportunity and built around individual agency, merit, and initiative. It is justice individualized, not socialized or collectivized. Interestingly, there is also some recognition that this system may not always be just.[17] Although there is some disagreement about the extent

---

freedom (to compete and make choices) as its ultimate justification for state subsidy and support.

[15] See also Chapter 4 on redefining injury.

[16] This is consistent with points made above – both types of individualism adhere to economic measures whereby to assess the progress of not only position, but acceptance of ideology.

[17] One of neoliberalism's prominent architects, F.A. Hayek was not totally unsympathetic to what he might deem 'society's losers'. He even explicitly endorsed government action in providing some minimal level of welfare, particularly if it was geared toward making people fit for labour: '[T]here is no reason why in a society which has reached the

of and conditions for a safety net, both ends of the political spectrum concede the need for those whose 'deficiencies' or status would make individual responsibility unconscionable. In addition, individualistic ideology recognizes that there may be unfair obstacles or distortions in the system that inhibit competition or deny opportunity to those who are otherwise able to be equals. As a result, laws have been developed to prohibit discrimination based on certain 'protected' individual characteristics, such as gender or race. So, what has evolved is an individually focused politics that assumes fundamental equality and glorifies liberty and autonomy – one that is sceptical of governmental authority and action, even though it may also concede the necessity of incorporating a safety net and anti-discrimination remedies for those unfortunate few unable to realize the system's full potential.[18]

---

general level of wealth which ours has attained the first kind of security should not be guaranteed to all without endangering general freedom .... [T]here can be no doubt that some minimum of food, shelter, and clothing, sufficient to preserve health and the capacity to work, can be assured to everybody': F.A. Hayek, *The Road to Serfdom* (Routledge 1944). This labour-ready purpose for social welfare benefits reflects other neoliberal concepts, such as the language of 'welfare dependency' and 'moral hazard', which played an important role in undermining the extension of welfare policies: Hayek, *Road to Serfdom*. In fact, by the 1990s President Clinton declared that the era of big government was over and that '[t]oday, we are ending welfare as we know it ....': see Barbara Vobejda, 'Clinton Signs Welfare Bill Amid Division' (1996) *The Washington Post*, August 23, https://www.washingtonpost.com/wp-srv/politics/special/welfare/stories/wf082396.htm. For more information about the stereotypes and condemnations associated with welfare reform that took place in the mid-1990s, see Martha L. Fineman, 'Images of Mothers in Poverty Discourses' (1991) 274(2) *Duke Law Journal* 274. For an analysis on the elderly and social security, see Martha Albertson Fineman, ' "Elderly" as Vulnerable: Rethinking the Nature of Individual and Societal Responsibility' (2012) 20 *Elder Law Journal* 71.

[18] In regard to justice, political philosopher Philippe Van Parijs asserts that any defensible conception of justice must be liberal and egalitarian, explaining that he means 'liberal in the philosophical sense of professing

Now, contrast that contemporary vision and set of aspirations with the UN report's discussion of the history of the term 'social justice'. It describes a very different aspiration, one with the ambitious goal of defining the just 'organization of

> equal respect for the diversity of the conceptions of the good life that are present in our pluralistic societies': see Philippe Van Parijs, 'Social Justice and the Future of the Social Economy' (2015) 86(2) *Annals of Public and Cooperative Economics* 191–7. This conception of social justice is rooted in the economic and built around the individual. I do not mean to suggest that there is anything inherently wrong with concern for diversity or pluralism or, for that matter, with a goal of equal opportunity. I do, however, want to assert that such a focus is a theoretical and political problem when it totally eclipses the needs, functioning, and nature of society, and makes the individual the only relevant measure for justice. The realm of the social becomes blurred, if not completely dissolved, in what might better be described as individual economic justice. In regard to defining equality, Van Parijs clearly explained that equality is not to be interpreted to mean equivalence in outcome, and this is true whether what is distributed is happiness, income, wealth, health, or power. For him, inequalities in distribution can be justified in two ways. First is the principle of personal responsibility under which inequalities do not violate an egalitarian mandate if they are byproducts of pursuit of individual actions, provided there is what he terms 'real freedom'. This idea of real freedom is a central (and individually focused) theme in Van Parijs' work, although it is not fully explained. Sometimes he seems to indicate that real freedom equates with opportunity and is something to be fairly distributed: 'Equality is not a matter of equalizing outcomes, it is a matter of equalizing opportunities, possibilities, real freedom.' One would assume that this distribution of opportunity as constituting real freedom would have something to do with state action, but it is not clear what that action is or what its objectives are. However, it does seem clear that Van Parijs' conception of the state's proper role is a thin one and limited to the provision of opportunity, which one assumes means monitoring discrimination and exclusion. Presumably, any state interference with outcome would compromise this generalized access to real freedom, a conclusion buttressed by the articulation of his second principle, which is efficiency: '[W]e should not try to equalize at all cost …. [J]ustice is not about strict equality even of possibilities, but rather about the sustainable maximization of the minimum – the maximin – about making the real

society', not merely opportunities for the individual in the face of evolving social circumstances. The concern was with 'the fair and compassionate distribution of the fruits of economic growth', which was to be accomplished by giving authority to pursue the common good to public institutions.[19]

This vision does not begin with the individual, presupposing an equality of agency and ability and a preference for choice, but recognizes that there is a primary need for governmental response to changing economic and social circumstances (in that instance the industrial revolution). It also recognizes that creating institutional contexts for processing these kinds of changes both enable and constrain individual actions and options across society.[20] It sees social justice as a concern with the structural arrangements for the *initial* as well as the ongoing distribution of societal benefits and burdens, an assessment of how society should construct the floor – the foundation or

---

freedom of those with least real freedom as great as sustainably possible.' Van Parijs' logic here exemplifies the ascendency of the individual over the social conception of justice. Justice is no longer grounded in the creation of broad social welfare projects, unless they target the poor or disadvantaged, or are directed at increasing business and entrepreneurial opportunities deemed likely to unleash economic growth and trickle down to communities. In fact, individual equality and liberty are all too often construed as barriers against state action, with such action seen as interfering with individual choices or autonomy. See further Martha Albertson Fineman, 'Vulnerability and Social Justice' (2019) 53 *Valparaiso University Law Review* 341.

[19] Justice and fairness conceived as a social not individual project – entwined with collective action and responsibility. Not privileging particular individuals or groups.

[20] As pandemic responses and climate change show, it is the concept of individual constraint that seems incomprehensible to the modern-day individualist ideologies. Such all-encompassing and universally impacting phenomena are not successfully approached as presenting primarily social problems to be solved through the imposition of necessary and just collective 'sacrifice', but as challenges to individual entitlements and potential infringements on individual rights.

'superstructure' of society — the base below which our primary social arrangements cannot be deemed just.

Significantly, in that early vision the floor was to be determined by considering the common good. And while that term was not defined, it does not appear to be the equivalent of our notion of individual rights. In fact, the idea of the separate, autonomous individual would seem to have been displaced by the concern for social justice — sidelined, at least initially, by the social arrangements and practices that would envelop and shape our collective lives (not only the lives of particular individuals or groups).[21] The specific social concern mentioned in the report was defining the way labour and capital (and the position of employee and employer) would be organized in the wake of the industrial revolution. And while that certainly included the interests of the individual worker in fair and reasonable terms and conditions in the workplace, those concerns were considered part of a larger effort to set out measures to ensure the just distribution across society, and its institutions, of the social rewards economic growth might bring.

---

[21] By contrast, contemporary moral or fairness arguments for policies aimed at redistribution based on broader conceptions of justice are easily disposed of using two argumentative tactics. First, the adoption of a notion of relativism, or cultural pluralism, emphasizes individual choice and renders social justice a matter of individual definition. This manoeuvre also locates the ultimate responsibility with the individual, who must choose what is best for him, as well as determining how to achieve it. Second, the appeal to economic efficiency positions cost–benefit analysis as the ultimate standard for defining public policies. For those who recognize that sometimes pursuing social justice will be economically inefficient, this move to market principles is perverse. Social justice advocates need a vocabulary that does not privilege the economic over all else as the measure of acceptable social policy initiatives — one that sets out a logic emphasizing the social dimension of justice, recovering the notion of a collectively determined and realized sense of the public good. In other words, we need something like Vulnerability Theory.

This broadly collective approach to social justice recognizes the ways that fundamental structural arrangements affect not only specific individuals or groups, but also the wellbeing of families and communities. Importantly it also recognizes the often overlooked important and independent state interest in its ability to establish, secure, and reproduce society and its institutions, values, and practices. In any case, the concern at this fundamental stage was not with making adjustments or adaptations to a system that was considered just because we discovered deviations caused by individual misconduct, such as discrimination. The concern was with the preliminary question of what logic and values should control the creation of basic social structures.

My question after reading the report was whether it would be possible to get back to that collective conception of social justice. I think this question is particularly pressing in view of our dangerously inadequate responses to collective threats like the COVID-19 pandemic or the climate crisis, as well as various other more localized pending disasters that seem to require some sort of common good response. The UN report is pessimistic on this point. For some, of course, the question would be: why would we even want to try? Why bring up questions of public good when it is primarily our individual interests that are at stake? I optimistically assume that there is at least some interest on the part of some scholars in developing a richer conception of social justice than that which currently exists, which brings me back to Vulnerability Theory.

## 3.3 Vulnerability Theory and social justice

The idea of the vulnerable (rather than the liberal) legal subject has the power to disrupt the logic of the current fixation on individual choice and personal responsibility. It does so by accepting and theoretically centring in on a more inclusive and realistic political legal subject in determining what can and should be our idea of fundamental state responsibility.

This legal subject must recognize the physical and societal implications of vulnerability, as well as the social dependency that our vulnerability inescapably entails.

This vulnerable subject would replace the autonomous, independent, liberty-seeking individual that currently dominates policies and politics, thus also bringing to the forefront the concept of resilience and questions of appropriate state responsibility.

### 3.3.1 Resilience

Resilience is centrally important in vulnerability analysis. While there is no position of invulnerability, fortunately there is resilience. Resilience is provided by those assets or resources provided by the material, cultural, social, and existential resources that allow us to respond to vulnerability over the life course.

Resources can come in material forms, such as the goods and services we can acquire with wealth produced through participation in business, economic, and financial systems. They also have non-material forms. For example, it is within families or social networks that we can gain the relational or social resources that provide us with emotional and psychological stability, as well as preparation for social interactions. 'Human capital' is a term often used to describe the knowledge/capability resources that can come from education or training, as well as work experience and professional development. Existential resources can be built through religious affiliation or emerge from engaging with philosophical or ascetic ideas that provide a sense of meaning and belonging in life. Environmental resources also are critical. The condition of both the built and natural environment profoundly affects both individual and communal health and wellbeing.

Ultimately, resilience allows an individual to survive or recover from harm or setbacks that inevitably occur over the life course. Resilience also supplies the resources that allow individuals to take risks – form relationships, undertake transactions, take advantage of opportunities – confident that, if they fail the challenge or meet unexpected obstacles, they are likely to have the means and ability to recover. In other words, resilience allows us to respond to life – not only to survive, given our vulnerability, but to thrive within the circumstances in which we find ourselves.

### *3.3.2 Social institutions and relationships*

However, and this is a most important aspect of resilience, human beings are not born resilient. Rather, resilience is produced over time and within social institutions and under societal conditions, institutions, and conditions over which individuals may have little or no control. Importantly in this regard, resilience-conferring institutions operate both simultaneously and sequentially in society. Failure to successfully build resources in one stage of life can fundamentally affect the ability of an individual to succeed in another. So, an inadequate education will impair the ability to secure employment and accumulate material goods, which will also affect outcomes further down the life course, like health, family formation, and prospects in old age. Movement into a new phase of life may depend on successful accomplishment of the tasks set in the earlier stage and it may be difficult for an individual to recover if that accumulation does not happen.

The fact that institutions operate simultaneously is also significant when thinking about resilience. Resilience gained through one institutional or relational arrangement can offset or mitigate disadvantages in another (and vice versa). A strong family, for example, can compensate for a weak education, while a violent or abusive family can undermine the advantages of a strong education. Again, these institutions act in tandem.

Lastly, because resilience is inevitably socially produced – generated and accumulated within social institutions – it must be located within a well-developed notion of state responsibility.

These institutions are creatures of law. Law brings them into existence and establishes and monitors the terms and consequences of their operation (that is, the family, the corporation, the healthcare/financial/educational systems, and so on). The social role and function of these institutions are currently cloaked by various ideological constructs: the free market, small government, individual autonomy and liberty, agency, family privacy, and efficiency. These constructs suggest the state be restrained, so as to not intervene or interfere with the innovation of the free market or the magic of the private family.

So, one task for a social justice scholar is to show the myriad ways in which the state actually creates, maintains, supports, and subsidizes these institutions – whether they are labelled public or private – through its laws and policies, recognizing that, at best, they are semi-private. And even that category should not mean the abdication of state responsibility, as it often does.

## 3.4 Social justice questions from a vulnerability perspective

In our scholarship, and in our political and policy discussions, we should be asking: what sort of justice is delivered by our tax, corporate, and finance laws. What are the social effects of the rules that govern families and the health and educational systems and other systems? Are there unjust, inequitable subsidies and privileges for some, which are delivered through these social institutions and relationships? What are the burdens and disadvantages placed on others? And how does all of this tell what the impact is going to be on society?

In undertaking this analysis, the primary focus would initially be on the organization and operation of the institutions, not on particular individuals within those institutions. This argument acknowledges that societal institutions affect us all. If they are inadequately regulated, they are susceptible to capture, corruption, decay and failure, and this can have serious implications for the wellbeing of society, as well as the individual.

Social justice requires a responsive (and justly active) state, one that is organized to be responsive and attentive to the dependency of the vulnerable subject and actively pursue the public or common good in the creation and monitoring of social institutions and relationships.

In the end, what does seem clear is that what constitutes social justice is a political judgment derived from the application of political concepts and, as such, it is susceptible to change and challenge over time. We have seen that happen already. And change is the goal of Vulnerability Theory, which seeks to provide a framework for critical analysis to, in fact, promote a better situation for everyone in society.

# FOUR

# Lecture 3 – Injury

## Introduction to Lecture 3

This lecture considered the limited ways in which injury or harm is understood, particularly in US political and legal culture. The concern is with the inability of contemporary constitutional or political theory to interpret the failure of collective or state action as constituting a harm worthy of recognition and compelling remedial action. In this lecture, I am interested in the norms and values that inform the principles governing the exercise of action and restraint on the part of the state when it acts as sovereign and in its relationship with individuals as political or legal subjects.

The idea that constitutional injury or harm can be caused by state inaction is not well-developed in US political and legal culture. Indeed, the norms and values informing our ideas of appropriate actions on the part of the state, as well as defining the corresponding entitlements of political or legal subjects, are firmly anchored in the principle of non-intervention or inaction. The spectre of state or public interference with individual privacy or liberty interests haunts the American constitutional order and shapes what is perceived as constituting injurious state action. Restraints on the state are viewed as imposed by the terms of the social contract, which is often referred to as creating a system of 'negative rights'. By contrast, 'positive rights' would place affirmative obligations on the state (and/or others) to act in the interest of others.[1] American jurisprudence, as it has developed within the framework of negative rights, elevates the ideal of individual liberty over any robust sense of the necessity for collective or substantive equality.[2]

This distinction between negative and positive rights is popular among some normative theorists, especially those with a bent toward libertarianism. As a result, many approaches to state responsibility tolerate (and even condone) state disregard for or abandonment and neglect of basic human needs. Profound inequalities in circumstances, status, and wellbeing are accepted – even justified – by reference to individual responsibility. Proposed remedial and altruistic responses are deflected with warnings about the addictive dependency asserted to be intrinsic to the highly stigmatized system of welfare currently in place in the US. State neglect of the situation of those individuals living in poverty or suffering under social, economic, and material disadvantage is not seen

---

[1] A negative right is a right not to be subjected to an action of another person or group – a government, for example – usually in the form of abuse or coercion. A positive right is a right to be the recipient of an action by another person or group. In theory, a negative right forbids others from acting against the right holder, while a positive right obligates others to act with respect to the right holder. The holder of a negative right is entitled to non-interference, while the holder of a positive right is entitled to provision of some good or service.

[2] A social contract is defined as '[a]n implicit agreement among the members of a society to cooperate for social benefits, for example by sacrificing some individual freedom for state protection': (2016) *Oxford English Dictionary*, https://www.oed.com/dictionary/social-contract_n?tab=etymology-paywall#21924478, accessed September 26, 2024. The documents comprising the American social contract – the Declaration of Independence, the Bill of Rights, and the Constitution with its federalist structure and enumerated powers – uphold individual liberty at the expense of a more substantive equality. The Bill of Rights enumerates some specific prohibitions or limitations on state action. The Constitution also imposes duties of equal protection and due process, and there are legal remedies for individuals.

as requiring legal or political remedy. Quite the contrary: state inaction is typically viewed as the appropriate manifestation of state restraint in the face of individual liberty or autonomy rights that condemn any move toward the redistribution of private wealth or property. 'Private' structures, such as the family, market, charity, or the workplace, are designated as the prime mediating institutions to provide for the needs of individuals.

This lecture employs Vulnerability Theory and asks us to consider the negative results of state inattention and inaction on individuals (and society itself) as an injury – an injury inflicted by state inaction. It argues that the disregard of impoverishment, disenfranchisement, alienation, and exploitation of substantial numbers of individuals within and through the systems of law and politics rises to the level of 'gross negligence' on the part of the state. It further argues that such neglect should be understood as the 'social-contractual injury'. The state's inaction effectively institutionalizes subordination and inequality.

★★★

## Lecture 3 – Injury

I want to begin with a brief recap of the previous lectures. The first step in a vulnerability analysis is to recognize that the basic political or legal subject is not intrinsically rational, autonomous, or independent, but vulnerable across the life course. We reach this conclusion by reasoning from the physical and social realities of the body (reasoning from the body) and thus understanding the inevitability of developmental, social, and environmental change and their implications for both our physical and social wellbeing.

We then argue, from this initial observation, that we must replace the liberal autonomous legal subject with the vulnerable subject in assessing law, policy, and politics. This leads to the second step in the analysis: situating the complex, comprehensive, evolving vulnerable subject within the institutional arrangements upon which we are all inevitably dependent throughout life.[3]

A focus on these social relationships broadens our attention beyond the situation of the individual to the institutional structures of society that affect everyone, structures in which we inevitably live our day-to-day lives. We recognize that these institutional arrangements are profoundly shaped by the ways in which the state initially either exercises or abdicates its governing authority and power, as well as how it defines its duty to monitor these arrangements once they are established. That brings us to today and the question of how we should understand injury from a vulnerability perspective.

## 4.1 Individual and collective harm

Now certainly the concept of injury would include traditional sorts of individual harm that are captured by criminal, contract, torts, and other areas of law. It would also recognize governmental obligation to address distortions in the implementation of policies caused by discrimination and ensure

---

[3] It is this second step, which involves a normative or political analysis, that should occupy most of a vulnerability analysis. Unfortunately, perhaps because the theory is relatively recent in development, most of the discussions tend to focus on the definitional question and universal nature of vulnerability. As several of my students have noted, the logic of universal vulnerability is compelling, but the emotional acceptance of its implications for them as individuals – the insecurity of their own reality – is difficult to fully accept. This reflects the hegemony of both the extreme individualism fostered by libertarian notions of freedom, autonomy, independence, and attachment to discrimination or other particularized notions of individual (or group) injury as the appropriate way to argue for state action (to correct a recognized, particular harm).

equality under the law. But is something more suggested by a vulnerability analysis (in the way of understanding injury)?[4]

In today's suggested readings, there are excerpts from several of my earlier articles in which I actually anticipated the injury question, although I did not directly address it in vulnerability terms.[5] Nonetheless, I think it is interesting to see how these issues and questions have evolved, particularly in relation to Vulnerability Theory.

These early pieces develop the relationship between dependency and care work and the concept of 'social debt'.[6] During the late 1990s, my work was focused on the institution

---

[4] The answer to this question is obviously 'yes'. The purpose of the first two lectures was to suggest that a focus on the individual should (at least initially) be replaced by a consideration of the collective or aggregate circumstances or situations in an effort to articulate a comprehensive notion of state or collective responsibility.

[5] These earlier articles encompassed the notion of injury from a failure of collective or governmental response. They were firmly anchored in the concepts that evolved as part of my work within the Feminism and Legal Theory Project, which I founded in 1984 at the University of Wisconsin. That project, which was attended over the years by many important scholars actively involved in feminist legal theory from an interdisciplinary perspective, viewed feminist legal theory through an institutional lens, informed by the principles of the Law and Society movement, rather than in purely identitarian notions. An archive consisting of written materials, as well as videos of workshops spanning 40 years of this work, which also ultimately forms the foundations for vulnerability theory, are available at Emory University Law School's MacMillan Library. More information at: https://library.law.emory.edu/collections/feminism-and-legal-theory.html. A less comprehensive set of materials can be accessed through HeinOnline's Women and the Law (Peggy) database, https://libguides.heinonline.org/women-and-the-law.

[6] 'Cracking the Foundational Myths' (2000) 8(1) *American Journal and Law and Social Policy* 13; 'The Inevitability of Dependency and the Politics of Subsidy' (1998) 9 *Stanford Law and Policy Review* 89; 'The Nature of Dependencies and Welfare Reform' (1996) 36 *Santa Clara University Law Review* 287; 'Masking Dependency: The Political Role of Family Rhetoric' (1995) 81 *University of Virginia Law Review* 2181.

of the family and the nature and functions of family law. As a self-proclaimed feminist scholar, I was concerned with caretaking and how we might achieve gender equality in the family context. These early articles complicated the concept of dependency as it was then (and perhaps now) understood.

The pieces were written as a reaction to the contemporary debates about welfare reform that were raging at the time in the US.[7] The accusation was that governmental support for families had created what were called 'cycles of dependency' in which generation after generation was caught in a welfare trap. This was used as an argument against the provision of welfare. My arguments at that time directly confronted the issue of dependency, looking at the role of the family in managing biological or developmental dependency.

## 4.2 Dependency and injury

I began with the observation that individual dependency on care is universal, an inevitable developmental stage. But I then added that there were several other layers of dependency that were in need of theoretical attention. One, considered in Lecture 1, was that of 'derivative dependency'.[8] If you recall,

---

[7] The dependency debates were manipulated by politicians such as Ronald Reagan and his characterization of the 'welfare queen' who purportedly manipulated the system in reprehensible criminal ways, but also by liberal politicians, such as Daniel P. Moynihan who articulated the cycles of dependency argument. See Moynihan Report to the 1986 presentation of the problems of the Black family in Bill Moyers' documentary, 'The Vanishing Family: Crisis in Black America.' See Daniel P. Moynihan, *The Negro Family: The Case for National Action* (Office of Planning and Research, United States Department of Labor 1965), https://web.stanford.edu/~mrosenfe/Moynihan's%20The%20Negro%20Family.pdf; 'The Vanishing Family: Crisis in Black America' (1986) CBS television broadcast, January 25, transcript on file at University of Miami Law Review; see also Daniel P. Moynihan, *Family and Nation* (Harcourt 1986).

[8] See Chapter 2.

derivative dependency is the dependency of the caretaker on resources in order to effectively accomplish their caretaking work. However, I also pointed out the often overlooked but significant reality that society is also derivatively dependent. Specifically, the wellbeing of society (and its individual members) is fundamentally dependent upon the caretaking work assigned to the private family.

The allocation to the family of primary responsibility for dependency, as well as the care work it requires, created what I called a collective or societal debt. I argued that each and every member of society was obligated by this debt. As a collective debt, it transcends individual circumstances. In other words, we need not be elderly, ill, or children any longer to be held individually responsible for this social debt. Nor can we satisfy or discharge our collective responsibility within our individual, private families. Merely being financially generous with our own mothers or duly supporting our own wives will not suffice to satisfy our share of this societal debt generally owed to all caretakers. I noted that this care work was society preserving – essential work that sustained and reproduced society. Just as individual dependency needs must be met if an individual is to survive, collective dependency needs must be met if a society is to survive and perpetuate itself. The mandate that the state (or collective society) respond to dependency, therefore, is not a matter of altruism or empathy (which are individual responses often resulting in charity), but fundamental and communal (mandatory). Without aggregate caretaking, there could be no society, so we might say that it is caretaking labour that produces and reproduces society.

These early articles also emphasized the importance of societal institutions that serve as mediating structures or legally contrived mechanisms for fulfilling what was ultimately a collective or state responsibility.[9] In this context, the private

---

[9] This focus on institutions as mediating structures, facilitating and channelling social or collective responsibility also anticipated, although

family served as the preferred policy solution to the dilemma of care, but there was a design flaw. This family was conceptualized as ideally self-sufficient and independent, not in need of subsidy or governmental transfers. In other words, this constructed private family was designed to privatize dependency (to make private this collective debt).

These articles also pointed out the empirical fallacy and logical inconsistency within that aspiration of privatization. I now realize that in these dependency arguments I was actually making a claim about what constitutes injury, although it was not expressed as such at the time. The injuries were to the family as an institution, because a lack of state support made it difficult to fulfil its function. There were also injuries to the caretaker. These injuries resulted from the failure of society to acknowledge and justly value, accommodate, and compensate the labour of caretakers. As a result, the burdens and sacrifices arising from undertaking care work were borne primarily by the family as an institution in the first instance, and within that family by those who assumed the social role of caretaker.

The harsh implications of this arrangement for the individuals undertaking this essential social work were ignored and obscured by dominant family politics and policies. This constitutes an injustice – the infliction of injury through governmental policy and preference.[10] I made the analogy to the armed services, which are established to attend to the collective need for national defence. But delegation (at least in that context) was not the same thing as abandonment of collective or state responsibility. The armed services were simultaneously structured as both the responsibility of only

---

it did not fully articulate. Vulnerability Theory's attention to institutional rather than individual responsibility.

[10] The injuries are the result of both action (the privatization of the family) and inaction (the neglect of responsibility for and recognition of the necessary work done by and within the privatized family).

some designated members (volunteers or draftees) and of all members of society (taxpayers, voters, and politicians).

I argued that the imposition of this dual and complementary responsibility is consistent with our deeply held beliefs about how rights and obligations are accrued and imposed in a just society. Collective obligations have both an individual and a collective dimension. Certain members of society may be recruited, volunteered, or even drafted, but they have a right to be compensated for their services from collective resources. They also have a right to the necessary tools to perform their assigned tasks and to guarantee that they will be protected by rules and policies that facilitate their performance. Caretakers should have an analogous right to have their society-preserving labour supported and facilitated.

In this context, I also attacked the delusion of independence that permeates the policy discussions around the question of subsidy. Subsidy was a highly stigmatized term at that point, indicating a lack of independence and self-sufficiency by the individual who is subsidized. My counterargument followed from the idea of a collective debt owed as a result of the benefits we all gain from the privatized family and care work. If that is true, then it seems clear that we all live subsidized lives. Sometimes the benefits we receive are financial, such as in governmental direct transfer programmes to certain individuals like farmers or sugar growers. Other subsidies are not explicitly so, such as the benefits given in tax policy. Caretaking within the private family illustrates that a subsidy can also be non-monetary, unrecognized, and ignored in policy debates as typically is the subsidy provided by the uncompensated labour in caring for dependency needs.

If the caretaking subsidy argument is accurate, it should be clear that all of us receive both monetary and non-monetary forms of subsidies throughout our lives. The interesting question in our subsidy-shaped society has to be why it is that only some subsidies are stigmatized. They are stigmatized when they are called welfare created to support the struggling individual but termed 'investments', 'incentives', or 'earned' when they are supplied to society's job creators or market actors.[11]

The second excerpt relevant to this lecture introduces something called the 'still face paradigm'.[12] This piece from 2017 was written after I had done a considerable amount of work on Vulnerability Theory. This piece more explicitly explores the relationship between the failure of the state to act and the idea of injury on both an individual and a societal level.

I described the results of a psychology experiment designed to observe the significance of interaction between mothers and their infants. As part of the experiment, the mothers were instructed to play with their children as usual, but to make their facial expression 'flat and neutral'. In other words, they were not to show any emotion or response to the infant. This feigned indifference was the very opposite of the typical

---

[11] In particular, I was struck by two quasi-economic responses to the point that caretakers should be compensated or accommodated. I refer to one as the 'Porsche Preference'. This argument states that if someone prefers a child, this preference should not be treated differently than any other choice (like the choice to own a Porsche). Society should not subsidize either preference. I hope the society-preserving nature of children helps to distinguish that preference from the whim of the auto fan. The other argument I label the 'efficiency and exploitation' model. This argument is really nothing more than the assertion that, if women allow themselves to be exploited as unpaid or underpaid caretakers, that is then the most efficient resolution for the problem of caretaking and dependency and should not be disturbed. Aside from the fact that this arrangement is not working and that it results in massive poverty and other social ills, this type of argument also demonstrates how little economics has to offer to considerations of justice.

[12] Martha Albertson Fineman and Silas W. Allard, 'Vulnerability, the Responsive State, and the Role of Religion' in H. Springhart and G. Thomas (eds), *Exploring Vulnerability* (Vandenhoeck & Ruprecht 2017) 81.

attentive and responsive interactions most mothers have when playing with their babies. The experiment was to assess how the infants responded.

The researchers observed that the infants became anxious when the mothers presented a 'still face'. They noted that they 'showed ever-greater signs of confusion and distress' as the mother neglected to respond. This was followed by an actual turning away from the mother, eventually resulting in what the researchers said were signs of hopelessness and depression in the infants. The study indicates that these findings were consistent with the developmental literature that argues human beings need those who care for them to be responsive in order to feel secure and able themselves to develop empathy and compassion. In other words, these important social skills are learned through our early interactions with those who care for us.

Interestingly, one commentator on the study suggested that the still face paradigm revealed in the experiment served also as a metaphor for adult life in contemporary society. He argued that the helplessness observed in the infants reflected the experience of many people as they interact with the most important institutions in their lives, including the government. Inattentiveness and indifference could inflict widespread damage on an individual's psyche, causing distress, anger, and hopelessness, as well as something he labelled as 'status-anxiety'. There was also a suggestion that the individual injury to the psyche from inattention might have societal consequences, causing trust in others to break down, which, since trust is a component of an effective and functioning society, would have negative societal implications.

## 4.3 Injury and state responsibility

Vulnerability Theory is a legal and political theory, not one based in psychology, but we can and should learn from such interdisciplinary insights.[13] The still face research can provide a poignant metaphor representing both the essential nature of our dependence on care from others and the despondency and dislocation that can happen when that care fails to happen or is unresponsive and inadequate. Consistent with Vulnerability Theory's view of the individual as inescapably dependent on society, the still face metaphor reminds us that we are social beings, inescapably enmeshed in social relations and institutions, and that there are consequences when those institutions and relationships fail us.

In this regard, I also find it useful to recall Elie Wiesel on the nature of indifference. As you may recall, he reflected that: 'The opposite of love is not hate, it's indifference. The opposite of art is not ugliness, it's indifference. The opposite of faith is not heresy, it's indifference. And the opposite of life is not death, it's indifference.'[14] Vulnerability Theory asks us to consider indifference as injury – harms that occur when a society is unresponsive or inadequately responsive to human needs, aspirations, and anguish.

Vulnerability Theory thus locates indifference within the context of state or collective responsibility, not only with the individual. That responsibility arises from the fact that human beings are inevitably dependent on societal institutions and

---

[13] The 2023 UNICEF analysis emphasizes the vital role of responsive caregiving in early childhood. In doing so, it aligns with the still face metaphor, showing how the lack of responsiveness in care can have long-term developmental impacts. Such empirical evidence supports the theoretical arguments that Vulnerability Theory offers to argue society must recognize and prioritize fundamental dependency needs. See more in: United Nations Children's Fund (UNICEF), *Early Childhood Development. UNICEF Vision for Every Child* (UNICEF 2023), https://www.unicef.org/media/145336/file/Early%20Childhood%20Developm ent%20-%20UNICEF%20Vision%20for%20Every%20Child.pdf.

[14] Elie Wiesel as quoted in *US News and World Report*, October 27, 1986.

relationships throughout life.[15] That dependence mandates the formation of social institutions such as the family, as well as the organization of the community, government, and other sources for systems of rules and processes. While these arrangements serve the needs of the individual, they must also be designed to facilitate the successful running and reproduction of society. It is through the creation of these institutions, relationships, and rules that shape the individual's everyday life, that society not only gains the authority to govern but also the legitimacy necessary to perpetuate itself. In other words, the collective has a duty to be responsive to the actual needs of the individual – to our vulnerability and dependency.

Indifference on the part of the governing structures of society to the realities of the human condition constitutes a profound injury, an injury inflicted by a disregard and abdication of responsibility that of necessity must attach to the essential governing structures that construct and maintain society. The manifestation of this injury is found in the incoherent construction of the contemporary political and legal subject and the feeble sense of governmental responsibility it mandates.

Contemporary Western societies typically emphasize the values of individualism and autonomy and reflect an impractical faith in free-market principles to provide for the collective welfare. In fact, in the mid-twentieth century, scholars and philosophers such as Hayek and Friedman defined

---

[15] This is an existential argument that has some resonance in sociobiology and other theories that take seriously the implications of embodiment and its limitations for the survival of the individual. According to Edward O. Wilson, author of *Sociobiology: The New Synthesis* (Harvard University Press [1975] 2000), sociobiology is 'the systematic study of the biological basis of all social behavior'. However, Vulnerability Theory goes beyond the biological (embodiment) to focus instead on the varied and distinct processes whereby systemic or governmental rules are developed in response to these biological realities, and to assess these structural innovations and the processes that produce them that distinguish the human from other animals.

injury itself as state intervention.[16] In other words, the state's intervention and action were themselves considered an injury, thus enshrining indifference as a fundamental principle. Non-intervention essentially became constitutionally mandated in this type of neoliberal market-oriented society. Faith in privatization and the social benefits of efficiency have not only prevailed but triumphed over more collectively responsive models of society since that time.

What happens to social cohesion and trust when the individual is held to expectations imposed by a regime of 'personal responsibility', tempered slightly by some recognition of 'individual rights' against state excesses? What damage is done to the social fabric of a society when the failure to thrive is blamed on the individuals, and the social institutions and relationships upon which we are all dependent are drained of the resources they need in order to provide constitutionally mandated equality of opportunity and access? What are the social and individual implications of a society built around competition, not compassion?

We should ask those politicians obsessed with austerity, low taxes, and privatization to imagine what lessons children learn when in the publicly funded or state schools they attend the material and equipment necessary for even a modestly adequate modern education are missing. How do these children understand their society's sense of justice and fairness when, at the same time they are experiencing deprivation they see a million-dollar sports complex (or some other symbol of societal indulgence) being constructed with the assistance of public resources?

This is not just an exercise to engage from a child's perspective. For everyone in society, the significant question should be how we understand and evaluate justice when

---

[16] Chapter 3 (Lecture 2) explores this in the context of discussing the concept of social justice.

the state acts (or fails to act) in seeming ignorance of the economic and social contexts in which individuals actually find themselves. What should be the response of those who are abandoned to their assumed autonomy, independence, and liberty in a system that privileges privacy and valorizes profit maximization over the provision of structures designed for a more generalized notion of societal wellbeing? What lessons are there for employees when their interests are disregarded as inefficient, and they and their concerns marginalized in a perverse and hollow rhetoric of contract, equality, and choice that totally disregards existing power inequality structured within the existing employment relationship by law? What is the recourse when the meagre rules that protect worker health and safety are vilified and ignored, evaded by multinational corporations with the assistance of law and the politicians who argue such protections are an unnecessary interference with free markets? What are there for all of us when those same corporations evade environmental protections, calling them inefficient and unnecessary restraints on a free market, leaving individuals to bear the health and other burdens that result in the name of growth and progress? If they are recognized, such injuries are all too often deemed aberrations and exceptions in a market system where we are all assured by those in positions of power that it is functioning in the interests of all.[17]

---

[17] The preceding catalogue of socially imposed injuries are explored in some detail in the series of books that collected essays given at workshops over the years showing how the theory might impact different areas of law and policy. These books are included in the Bibliography. The topics include essays using Vulnerability Theory to look at social institutions and relationships found in legal arrangements regarding employment, contract, property, corporations, and so on. The workshops were held at Emory University as part of the Vulnerability and the Human Condition programming that has grown and flourished since its formation in 2008. Videos of the presentations and discussions are available to researchers at the Vulnerability and Human Condition Archive at MacMillan Law Library.

I want to be clear that concern about the injury currently done by ignoring vulnerability and dependency in our neoliberal market system does not mean that the state can or should abolish, abandon, or neglect the market or any other social institution. In fact, quite the contrary. Vulnerability Theory teaches us that societal institutions and relationships are essential to both individual and societal wellbeing, and this would include the market and its institutions. These form a part of the overlapping social structures in which we gain resilience and upon which we depend throughout life.

What Vulnerability Theory demands is that we also remember that these institutions and relationships are not inevitable in their form or their function. They are, in fact, creatures of the state, brought into existence and empowered to act through law and policy. As such, they should be understood to be defined by and entangled with the concept of collective or social responsibility. These contrived institutional arrangements are the means or mechanisms whereby societal benefits and burdens are to be distributed. It is this role or function in society (this distribution and allocation role) that justifies them and the policies that we enact to sustain and support them.[18]

The problem is that these structures currently operate under this free-market ideology that results in them being considered private and thus beyond routine regulation.[19] However, in

---

[18] Figure 2.2 showing the symbiotic relationship and interdependence of institutions that is included at the end of Chapter 2 is relevant in this regard.

[19] The chameleon character of the market in this public/private scheme is interesting. It is cast as public vis-à-vis the family, but private vis-à-vis the state, seeming to gain the advantage of each category. In this regard, it is interesting to note that when the comparison is of market versus family, the 'private' sphere of the family is subject to heavy public regulation, mostly because it retains aspects of 'status' and is not governed by contract. In contrast, the 'public' arena of the marketplace is governed by bodies of designated 'private' law, such as contract. These contrary characterizations have ideological nuances.

considering the question of social or governing responsibility it is important to consider the possibility that the laws and policies that have brought these institutions into existence may unjustly privilege or benefit some individuals and groups and injure or disadvantage others.[20] Yet despite this possibility, under the misleading rubric of the private, such institutions are left generally unsupervised in their ongoing operations.

Disregard or indifference on the part of those who make and administer law to the possibility of alienation and exploitation of some individuals resulting from current societal arrangements should be recognized as an injury – an injury requiring intervention and action on the part of the state. A failure to act in the face of such dysfunction should be understood as constitutional in that it is an injury inflicted not only on individuals but on society itself. Such indifference would violate the very purpose for which the state is constituted and injure those for whom it is therefore responsible.

One compelling task that presents itself at this point in the twenty-first century for those who care about social justice is to address the abdication of state responsibility for institutional relationships by modern societies that seem much more attuned to the needs of the market than to the individuals who must operate within it. What language and concepts can challenge the relentless rhetoric of individual independence that also glorifies the idea of personal responsibility? How can we articulate compelling arguments supporting the recognition of a collective responsibility: one that does not revert to the

---

[20] In noting the possibility of group advantage or disadvantage, the groups are those defined in terms of their relative institutional relationships (see again Figure 2.2 at the end of Chapter 2). In other words, it is the allocation of responsibility, benefits, power, and privilege between the complementary social identities of employer/employee, doctor/patient, landlord/tenant and so on that would be of concern, not the traditional demographic identities that are the basis for anti-discrimination and equal protection analysis.

individualistic delusions of meritocracy, choice, liberty, and free or unencumbered markets as the only appropriate means to allocate social goods? How do we demand our governing policies and practices recognize and compassionately respond to the reality of human vulnerability and the inevitability of social dependency? These are the questions that Vulnerability Theory tries to address in articulating what should be understood as an ethic or culture of governmental responsibility that places the vulnerable subject at the centre of law and policy.

# FIVE

# Lecture 4 – Inevitable Inequality

## Introduction to Lecture 4

Equality as an overarching aspiration (like liberty and autonomy) is grounded on a particular uncontextualized vision of the individual and an impoverished sense of the human condition that distorts our aspiration for justice and our expectations for collective responsibility.

Beginning with the body, Vulnerability Theory brings the temporal dimension of the life course into consideration, altering and complicating any discussion of what is the appropriate nature and extent of state responsibility for the wellbeing of the individual. A life-course perspective provides important insights into the totality of the human condition, and forces us to confront the illusion of equality as an organizing aspiration for a truly just society. It also urges us to consider how changes in the body over time should affect the ways in which we define our social institutions and relationships.

This discussion of inevitable inequality is fundamentally a discussion about the function and nature of social institutions and relationships and the role they play in shaping the individual. This discussion is not focused on the demographic differences or variations among individuals that are the focus of traditional anti-discrimination models of justice, but on the developmental changes that occur within every body. These inherent differences, which are biological and developmental, emerging over time, are largely ignored in constructing traditional theories about the appropriate relationship between the state and the legal or political subject.

Ignoring these developmental differences and focusing only on an adult, fully functional legal subject allows theorists to elaborate grand notions of individual liberty and autonomy without having to confront the justice of the structuring of social institutions and relationships. The individual is considered independently, not as inevitably enmeshed in these legal structures that are the products of state action and form the infrastructure of everyday life.

Bringing developmental differences into the discussion of state responsibility is essential for fully understanding what is at stake in considerations of state responsibility. The social institutions and relationships of everyday life are legal and political constructs. As such, their design, function, and operation are the products of governmental processes. Vulnerability Theory would require that legislators, administrators, and other state actors have the vulnerable subject firmly in mind when shaping these social arrangements. It also shows why law and policy must recognize that state responsibility for the just operation of these essential social structures must ultimately remain a state responsibility.

★★★

## Lecture 4 – Inevitable Inequality

Several important points made in the first three lectures are relevant to this discussion on 'inevitable inequality'.[1]

---

[1] Equality as an overarching aspiration (like liberty and autonomy) is based on a particular uncontextualized vision of the individual and an impoverished sense of the human condition that distorts our aspiration for justice and our expectations for collective responsibility. By bringing a life-course perspective, as well as focusing on inevitable and derivative dependency and the essential role of law and social institutions, Vulnerability Theory forces us to confront the institutional and individual realities of inevitable inequality.

First, the political or legal subject in Vulnerability Theory is not conceptualized as intrinsically rational, autonomous, and independent, but rather embodied and thus vulnerable across the life course. This vulnerable subject is understood as unavoidably and inherently dependent throughout life on social institutions and relationships, which are the mechanisms for gaining essential resources and capacities (or resilience) that allow us to survive and even thrive given our vulnerability.

Recalling the second lecture, the Vulnerability Theory message is that these institutional arrangements should reflect a sense of social rather than (or in addition to) individualized and particularized group justice. It is also important to remember that in addition to shaping the lives of the individual, these structures provide the mechanisms and means for the reproduction of society itself. So, society has a profound interest in the success or failure of these institutions that transcends that of the individual.

We also emphasized in the last lecture one significant aspect of an institutional rather than individual framework: the focus of Vulnerability Theory is on the whole of society. Our concept of constitutional or fundamental injury should not be limited to instances of targeted discrimination or subordination of a specific individual or group, but should also incorporate the idea of collective injury that comes from the failure of state actors to assume responsibility for the injustice that marks many of the societal arrangements affecting us all.

In other words, with Vulnerability Theory, the concern in the first instance is with the routine ordering of society's foundational institutions. These institutions must be constituted as responsive to the often-conflicting multiplicity of needs and interests that are inherent in a complex and diverse society. Societal institutions, ideally, are designed to justly balance the inevitably diverse claims and concerns, and also consider all of the affected actors (including the state as a principal and vulnerable party). In other words, in a vulnerability analysis, there are typically multiple vulnerable subject positions that represent a range of divergent legitimate interests.[2]

## 5.1 The unstable individual – vulnerability and change

As a result of beginning our inquiry by reasoning from the physical and social realities of the body, a series of pragmatic questions arise in Vulnerability Theory related to the nature and implications of change that is certain. Beginning with the corporeal body rather than some abstract and decontextualized principle such as autonomy, we must address the relationship between inevitable changes in both the physical body (developmental and biological changes) and the social environments in which we are situated (changes in the institutional arrangements in which we are embedded) over time.

Such alterations in situations and circumstances (both positive and negative) often result in or generate a need for corresponding modifications in the social status and material circumstances of the vulnerable subject. It is also true that

---

[2] Vulnerability Theory's focus on the multiplicity of vulnerable subject positions challenges monolithic understandings of justice. By recognizing the diverse interests and needs encompassed within institutional arrangements, this framework underscores the complexity of societal dynamics and the imperative for inclusive policymaking interests that are encompassed within any institutional arrangement. Additionally, it is essential to consider the roles and conflicts between social identities and institutional roles, such as how the role of an employee might conflict with that of a parent. In a vulnerability analysis, it is the failure of institutional responsibility or design that becomes the topic of critical inquiry, not discrimination. Finally, Vulnerability Theory also emphasizes the importance of understanding that these institutions are shaped by law and policy, and they must be designed to address the universal needs of the vulnerable subject. These institutions, whether public or private, are human creations that can and should be modified to ensure justice and resilience for all members of society.

the implications and effects of many changes profoundly affect societal as well as individual wellbeing. The dynamic and consequential reality of on-going change should have implications for the ways in which we approach and organize the principles guiding society and its institutions.[3]

These insights inform the next step in the vulnerability analysis, in which we situate the complex, comprehensive, dynamic vulnerable subject within the institutional arrangements upon which we are all inevitably dependent throughout life.[4] This step of placing the universal vulnerable individual within essential institutional contexts hopefully will encourage critical attention beyond the situation of the individual or specific group, and questions of discrimination or marginalization, to consider the entirety and complexity of the institutional positions and relationships established through law and policy.[5] The goal is to critically examine the nature

---

[3] The reality of change is an integral aspect of the idea of universal vulnerability both on an individual and institutional level. All individuals and all institutions are vulnerable to change, and change can be deemed positive as well as negative, or as inconsequential, depending on the nature of the change, the resources or resilience of the individual or institution, and the ability to incorporate or mitigate change. Of course, not all changes can be predicted or anticipated, but certainly many can (on both the individual level – such as aging and illness – or the institutional – such as economic shock or environmental challenges). In those situations where change is foreseeable, a responsive state would have put into place routine anticipatory remedial policies. All too often, however, such routine measures are not in place, and we are left to piecemeal or ad hoc measures in what is inappropriately treated an unexpected or unusual crisis situation.

[4] These social structures are the mechanisms through which we gain the resources (resilience) that allow us to move through, incorporate, and move beyond the changes in our situation and circumstances.

[5] As stated earlier, Vulnerability Theory recognizes the history of discrimination, as well as contemporary marginalization of specific groups. The suggestion is that, before we can effectively identify and address specifically directed failures or harms, it might be beneficial to

and specific operations of the essential institutional structures of society that affect everyone – those mundane structures in which we all are undeniably embedded and within which we must live our day-to-day lives.

## 5.2 Structuring institutional arrangements

Significantly, these institutional arrangements, although certainly products of culture and history, are ultimately also creatures of law. They are profoundly shaped by the rules and policies through which the state has interpreted and implemented its governing mandate. This mandate generally is understood as encompassing securing general health and welfare, maintaining social order, providing both public services and protection, and making necessary decisions regarding the allocation of resources, economic and otherwise. Ideally, these tasks are accomplished in ways that are consistent with preserving and perpetuating shared values and principles of society. Of course, there are divergent political and individual opinions as to how each of these goals should best be accomplished, as well as whether the list of categories of governmental concern is too narrow (or too broad). Although such disputes exist, it can be argued that it is the existential necessity to collectively attend to such essential communal objectives that actually legitimates the authority and power conferred on the governing system in society, justifying the constitution of the state in the first instance.

Consistent with this assertion, in the last lecture, we discussed the concept of injury and how the state's failure to act or its abdication of responsibility for certain of these governmental objectives might be considered a constitutional harm. For

---

see how the institution or relationship under scrutiny is structured in regard to ordering the universal or general status and power allocations.

example, an unwarranted or irresponsible delegation of state power or a failure to act in response to inequities or injustice might be described as an injury striking at the very source or foundation of state legitimacy, a violation of the very justification for state authority and power.

### 5.2.1 State responsibility and institutional construction

Vulnerability Theory as a legal or political theory is primarily concerned with questions of law and state authority or responsibility. It positions the state or governing authority as having both a foundational, communal, or social mandate to act in the public interest, along with a corresponding responsibility to consider individual wellbeing. And it also recognizes that sometimes these can conflict.

In fulfilling its responsibilities, the state constructs institutions and legal relationships that balance the general with the particular interest. These institutions can be separated into those that are explicitly instruments of governance – such as courts, administrative agencies, the military, and so forth – and those institutions that are designed to organize everyday life – such as the institution of the family or the workplace.

#### 5.2.1.1 Authoritative or despotic power[6]

In the first set of institutions, those explicitly governmental entities, the primary societal connection under consideration is the relationship between the state as sovereign power and the individual subject or citizen. The rules, procedures, and practices of these explicitly governmental institutions

---

[6] William J. Novak, 'The Myth of the "Weak" American State' (2008) 113(3) *American Historical Review* 752–72. Novak distinguishes between despotic power, the unchecked ruling ability of state elites, and infrastructural power, the state's capacity to implement policies and penetrate society.

are, of course, a major focus of critical theory, including Vulnerability Theory. These rules defining the state–institutional relationship, like the US Constitution, or announced by courts such as human rights courts in Europe, define the powers of adjudication or mediating issues involving state treatment of the individual. And the concerns with state governmental power that we see expressed in these courts include state infringement on individual rights, the necessity for equality of treatment, prohibitions against impermissible discrimination, and attention to individual agency and autonomy. One general shared fear is the possibility of over-reach by an authoritarian state and the resulting subordination of the individual. This is a persistent concern when we are looking at the direct relationship between state and individual.

Part of the health and welfare responsibilities of the state are also remedial or compensatory. Policies may provide a cluster of (exceptional or emergency) services and benefits that ensure some security for those individuals who are unable to access such benefits within the so-called private spheres of market and family. In conservative circles, the fear is that these social welfare entities or institutions create problems, particularly moral hazards that lead to the development of welfare dependency that destroys individual initiative and effort.[7] The state may act to address past discrimination or other failures to adhere to the mandate of equal treatment. In these contexts, there may be concerns on the part of recipients of such benefits about the possibility of being perceived as weak or inadequate in needing such assistance – concern with the possibility of stigma associated with policies deemed 'paternalistic'.

---

[7] There are also significant concerns mentioned in regard to the effect such services have on the budget and the 'problem' of imposing burdens on taxpayers.

*5.2.1.2 Institutional and infrastructural power*

Vulnerability Theory does not ignore these already well-analyzed institutions of explicit state power, but is more concerned with the under-theorized, separate set of institutions that shape the experience of everyday life, as contrasted with our so-called political or public life. These are the institutions that order the relationship between and among individuals in their societal roles or identities, such as parent/child, employer/employee, landlord/tenant, producer/consumer, and so on.

We are not accustomed to thinking of those relationships as contrived and constructed. They seem natural, organic in nature, primarily the products of familial love or market forces. However, in reality these structures, if they are legitimate, are products of governmental law and policy. Some sets of state-imposed coercive rules typically specify the nature, terms, and enforceable consequences of these relationships and ultimately shape individual options and aspirations. These institutions typically have some public purpose, even if it is not articulated as such. That purpose is instrumental in defining the rules that govern the institution, as well as those that impose institutionally derived duties, responsibilities, and prerogatives on individuals.[8]

These institutions of everyday life are often caught up and mischaracterized by a rhetoric of privatization, individual autonomy, and independence, reflecting the concerns of authoritative and potentially abusive governmental action.

---

[8] The rhetoric justifying state supportive policies toward corporations or other market entities is justified by their role in building the economy or providing material resources for individuals and families, objectives essential for any functioning society to achieve. The family as an institution is also considered necessary for the wellbeing of society in that it raises the young and takes care of the dependency needs of its members. The institutional identities defined by corporate or employment law or family law delineate the roles and responsibilities of individual actors such as the CEO or shareholder or the parent or spouse.

These infrastructural institutions thus are ensnared in a political vision that imagines the state as ideally peripheral to the structures of everyday life.

Vulnerability Theory, by contrast, acknowledges the centrality of state power and the necessity of state action in the constitution of everyday life.[9] In doing so, it seeks to articulate the principles, values, and norms that should guide the creation and maintenance of these essential societal institutions. Such an analysis begins by considering the societal purpose and expectation for these institutions in light of the situation and needs of the vulnerable subject. A recognition of the implications of human vulnerability and dependency would shape the principles to guide and define the state's decisions regarding the composition, influence, and functioning of these institutions, as well as ordering the relationship of the individuals within them.

It may well be possible to imagine the relevance of concepts such as autonomy and independence, or the ideal of a restrained state, in considering explicit exercises of state authority and defining the relationship between the individual and the state. However, in describing the individual-to-individual relationships integral to these institutions of everyday life (such as the family or workplace), concepts like autonomy and independence do not make empirical or intuitive sense. These terms envision divisible, binary, and contrasting relationships and interactions. By contrast, the infrastructural institutions of everyday life require an appreciation of their complexity, and attention to the need for balancing the multiplicity of, complementary and interlocking interests that are characteristic of social or institutional relationships.

---

[9] The delineation of institutional dynamics within Vulnerability Theory underscores its commitment to unravelling the intricate fabric of societal power structures. It reflects the theory's imperative to scrutinize both overtly political institutions and those governing the mundane aspects of everyday life.

Individualized normative concepts, such as autonomy and independence, have been derived from principles based on the flawed image of a solitary individual found in liberal theory rather than the dynamic and complex legal subject imagined in Vulnerability Theory. Autonomy and independence assume equivalently capable and socially distinct (even detached) legal actors, when the reality of social institutions is that corresponding relationships of asymmetric need and capability are at play. Such relationships are better understood as based on concepts of reciprocity, cooperation, complementarity, and contribution. Significantly, these also are often relationships of inherent inequality.[10]

Which brings me, of course, to the focus of today's discussion of inevitable inequality. Now, I want to be clear initially that to raise questions about the continued vitality or value of the equality/anti-discrimination paradigm is not to argue that equality and anti-discrimination laws and concepts are not important or have not been important. In fact, equality and anti-discrimination were unarguably essential steps in the evolution of a just society.

Prior to the mid-twentieth century, formal rules, as well as functioning norms, were built on assertions of fundamental differences among groups defined by age, gender, race, and other characteristics. These distinctive group categories also established a world of hierarchical, legalized identities in which some were susceptible to different, often demeaning treatment.

However, with the formal demographic distinctions now removed and equal access the norm, it becomes apparent that the problems in society often transcend discrimination

---

[10] One of the most significant contributions of Vulnerability Theory is found in its emphasis on the inherent inequality that typically defines everyday social relationships. Focusing on the inevitable inequality in such mundane (as contrasted with grand political) contexts compels us to address how such asymmetric, but essential social relationships should be justly arranged.

and exclusion from social institutions. That is, these are not problems of exclusion but problems with the institutions themselves. Indeed, there may be substantial problems with those institutions and their organization that are not revealed by a logic that flows from equality and anti-discrimination. Equality may, in fact, obstruct and create obstacles to the ability to remedy or even address current social realities (those not built on ideas of exclusion and difference).

An equality model or non-discrimination mandate certainly remains the appropriate response in many instances: one person, one vote, and equal pay for equal work are areas where equality seems clearly suitable. And, of course, it is essential when there is impermissible discrimination present to have anti-discrimination mandates and laws. However, equality may be an unjust objective when applied in situations of inescapable or inevitable inequality, where differing levels of authority and responsibility are not only appropriate but desirable, such as in defining the legal relationship between parent and child or even that of employer and employee.

Such relationships have historically been relegated to the private sphere of life – whether family or market – considered inappropriate areas for state regulation. When explicitly addressed, situations of inevitable inequality are typically handled either by imposing a fabricated equivalence between the individuals, or by declaring that the equality mandate does not apply because the individuals are positioned so differently.

An example of the imposition of fictitious equality in response to inevitable inequality can be found in the employment context, where a so-called contract is fabricated. This contract ignores the reality that the parties occupy unequal bargaining positions and have vastly different options to ameliorate and access alternative resources and options during economic downturns or other crises.

Similarly, an example of avoidance of the equality mandate can be found in the distinction drawn between the capabilities of children and adults. This difference is used to justify unequal state responsiveness and concern, where children are relegated to the confines of the private family and the whims of their parents.

Note that in both instances the state's responsibility for the ultimate justness of the institutional arrangement is minimized or obscured within the overriding framework of equality. The state is replaced by the social institutions it creates, thereby evading responsibility to the vulnerable subject, which from a vulnerability analysis is unacceptable. However, Vulnerability Theory begins its normative project for the state by reasoning from the body and recognizing the inherent dependency of the individual on social arrangement. Therefore, it is the articulated nature and function of social institutions and relationships that should command initial consideration. Although, in the abstract, these arrangements are essential to both individual and societal wellbeing, they are not universal or constant in the form and function they have been assigned. They are established to respond to universal needs, but the specific form an institutional structure ultimately takes will vary both across legal or political systems at any one time and over time within each system. Institutional arrangements are not natural or inevitable in form; they are human creations established through governing mechanisms using laws and policies, influenced by history, culture, power relations, and politics. Importantly, therefore, they are also susceptible to change.

These institutions and relationships are the primary mechanisms of distribution for social, economic, and political benefits and the way in which the state reproduces itself. These institutions and relationships are not isolated or independent, nor are their effects. They are essential to the success or failure of both the individual and society and profoundly affect the ways in which individuals experience universal vulnerability and whether individuals fail or succeed in their societally assigned tasks.

From a societal perspective, these institutions allocate privilege and power, distribute risk and reward, as well as subsidy and investment, and confer recognition and structure accommodation. However, distribution occurs along two dimensions. First, responsibility for distribution is spread across social institutions such as those forming family, market, healthcare, employment, and educational systems, done through regulations and administrative practices as well as constitutional jurisprudence. A significant allocation of responsibility for social reproduction is also accomplished by drawing a distinction and designating some institutions as public, while others are deemed private. Family is one way we privatize dependency, thus alleviating the state and the market from any primary responsibility. Second, within these social institutions, individual identities based on social functions are fashioned and enforced, resulting in paired and often complementary, but necessarily unequal, relationships such as parent/child, employer/employee, shareholder/consumer, doctor/patient, lender/borrower, and others. Through these identities, the social benefits and burdens of the reproduction of society are distributed to individuals using everyday law, such as contract, corporation, employment, family, criminal, and tort law, among others.

Vulnerability Theory explores the justice of these primary relationships of distribution from both institutional and social identity perspectives. However, Vulnerability Theory places the vulnerable subject at the centre of law, displacing the autonomous, independent liberal subject who now dominates theory. All too often, the burdens of individual and societal dependency are unjustly allocated to individuals within these societal identities, with risks and harms caused by everything from economic downturn to individual illness or misfortune being personalized rather than understood as institutional failures.

Furthermore, it is important to see how the state fails when social identities intersect unjustly. For example, how does the social role defined for the employee conflict with that defined for the parent? Often, the same person occupies both identities.

In a vulnerability analysis, it would not be the gender of the employee that would be initially relevant in this work–family conflict, but the societal tasks that are associated with the societal roles (that is, caretaker v employee). It is the failure of institutional responsibility or institutional design that becomes the topic of critical inquiry, not discrimination.

It is also important to see that the rhetorical seeds necessary for vulnerability or institutional criticism already exist within current political rhetoric. We should take seriously the arguments that politicians typically make for state subsidies and support of corporations and businesses. We should ask whether these entities are living up to the justifications that have been articulated for their state-subsidized and privileged existences. These market institutions are lauded as producing the economic wellbeing of society. The individuals controlling them are cast as wealth and job creators – entrepreneurs paving the path for economic growth and prosperity for the entire nation.

On the other hand, the family is praised for its role in raising the next generation of citizens and caring for those at the end of life. Parents are lauded for their self-sacrificing actions, and the self-sufficient (marital) family is valorized as both a moral and an economic ideal, uniquely qualified to attend to dependency and the needs of its members. These political and policy positions are based on the idea that these institutions, among others, have a central and essential role in organizing and reproducing society, as well as providing for the needs of the individuals.

This perception that institutions are necessary is correct from a vulnerability perspective. It also suggests that we must reject the current political dogma that places these institutions within a private sphere, distinguishing them from a public arena in which state action and responsibility are the norms.

This brings me to the final point of both this lecture and the series. The very public and pressing task, it seems to me, must be to design social institutions and relationships of everyday life that are responsive to the developmental and environmental realities of the vulnerable subject, which is the task that I hope to undertake using Vulnerability Theory. There is a lot of work to be done, and I hope some of you at least are interested in joining with us in trying to accomplish a more socially just society.

# SIX

# Institutionalizing the Individual

## Introduction to Chapter 6

As the preceding chapters have emphasized, the most significant theoretical focus of Vulnerability Theory is the concept of universal embodiment. It is an embodied (and therefore vulnerable) individual who encounters the myriad and inevitably shifting circumstances and situations of life. Rather than a distinct disadvantage or weakness attributed only to some individuals or present in distinct circumstances, vulnerability should be understood as a continuum of variations that together constitute the human condition.

In addition, the theory makes clear that the inherent dependency and limitations of the body necessitate reliance on functioning social institutions and relationships, which can foster individual resilience. Resilience is composed of social resources and relationships, which are the product of institutional policies and programmes when they are responsive and adaptive to the lived realities of the vulnerable subject.

As also emphasized in the lectures, far from being individual, variable, and particular traits or characteristics, both vulnerability (signifying our embodiment) and resilience (signifying our embeddedness) are the universal manifestations of the collective human condition. Combined, these insights form the foundation for Vulnerability Theory.

By institutionalizing the individual, we challenge the dominant legal and political narratives that prioritize individual autonomy and liberty over collective wellbeing. This approach brings the collective dimensions of justice into focus and mandates a broader and more inclusive conception of state responsibility, one that moves beyond merely safeguarding individual rights to actively shaping the social conditions necessary for resilience and wellbeing.

\*\*\*

## 6.1 The body

The body depicted in Vulnerability Theory is presented from an ontological or anthropological perspective, a corporeal entity that encompasses a wide and inclusive range of variations and adaptations. This distinguishes Vulnerability Theory from other critical analyses that focus on particular bodily variations, such as those concentrated on specific demographic categories or on distressed or disadvantaged social circumstances. While important in many circumstances, such specifically dedicated inquiries may risk overlooking the profound effects that distorted or problematic institutional arrangements can have on everyone in society. An analysis so limited may inspire solutions that address only the symptoms of an institutional inadequacy, while leaving untouched the underlying and more extensive structural distortions and defects.

There are advantages to initially assessing and addressing these infrastructural arrangements as they affect everyone. Such a systemic approach will often remedy (or at least alter) specific problems experienced primarily or disproportionately by subgroups of society (who may have been disproportionately affected). On the other hand, legal responses that offer mere inclusion or prohibitions against discrimination for only some can leave in place underlying inequitable and dysfunctional institutional arrangements, providing little more than an illusion of improvement.[1]

---

[1] If our concern is with a particularized subject who has been excluded or marginalized due to some set of assigned differences, what we naturally

To fully understand the implications of this universal approach to the body, we must also consider how these institutional structures interact within broader social and political frameworks.

## 6.2 The social and political implications of the universal

Building on the ontological understanding of the body and beginning with the universal or ontological body as a foundational theoretical concept would profoundly alter the focus and direction of contemporary political and legal doctrines. Challenging and displacing the long-held abstractions that have dominated these arenas, such a shift would require us to reconsider the very values and norms upon which our legal and political systems have been formed and justified. Moving away from a focus on an individualized approach to justice, we would have to define, incorporate, and accommodate the essential circumstances and requirements of the collective. This does not mean abandoning the individual. While the theoretical implication of the universal body in Vulnerability Theory certainly decentres the individual, by concentrating on the collective entity of all individuals, it paradoxically also brings greater clarity and attention to the physical and material conditions that form the reality of every individual.

Discrediting the practicality of the idealized abstract constructs of independence and autonomy, the universal subject of Vulnerability Theory would mandate a revisioning of the significance of the collective (and, ultimately, governance, law, and authority). The individual would be redefined as a legal and political subject which could only be adequately

---

seek are remedies such as prohibition or punishment of discrimination, as well as designing efforts to bring about inclusion. In these situations, the problem and the solution are both partialized and individualized, seldom bringing about structural adjustments or reform beyond the problem of exclusion as initially defined.

understood within the institutional contexts that our embodied vulnerability and resulting social dependency require. This redefinition of political and legal subjectivity is what is meant by the phrase 'institutionalizing the individual' – the individual in theory, as in life, must be placed within the complex and interrelated institutional contexts that actually define reality.

### 6.2.1 The institutionalized individual

A redefinition of the individual as inevitably embedded in social relationships and structures throughout life requires reframing questions of obligation and responsibility, as well as the mechanisms and principles for the social distribution of rewards and risks. The response of the state or the governing entity would of necessity be altered if we were to begin with the normalcy of vulnerability and dependency. Not only would problems be differently perceived, but the remedies sought would be more extensive and potentially transformative for society.

Concern with discrimination against particular individuals or groups is obviously very important, but it is also a quite different project than is the long-overdue effort to reform the conception of the universal liberal legal subject as the human avatar for legal and political theory. In a discrimination situation, the harm is a deviation from the legal mandate of equal treatment for all, not the skewed or distorted characterization of the human subject within these legal norms. Equality, in its conventional sense, is too narrow a concept to fully encompass the diverse ways in which individuals are affected by social, economic, and political forces.[2]

---

[2] Existing categories of discrimination are often expressed as rather simplistic binaries, drawing distinctions based on paired positions of difference such as male/female, Black/white, able/disabled. These distinctions tend to be viewed as fixed and unchanging over time, rather than perceived as historically limited constructs. As such they ultimately fail to incorporate and reflect the complexities of human variation or

However, there is a more significant problem with an analysis limited to only some in society. A primary focus on particular distinguishing categories can frustrate the search for a truly comprehensive and inclusive universal legal and political subject by deflecting attention from the societal role and functioning of institutions to the differences between individuals. With Vulnerability Theory, the inquiry should be into whether the structural arrangements established in society are responsive to the realities of the vulnerable human condition. Some important considerations include how social institutions are arranged in relation to each other and how they define and guide the institutional identities, expectations, and responsibilities of the individuals who are destined to live within them. These are among the issues that Vulnerability Theory seeks to explore, bringing social institutions and relationships firmly to the centre of critical analysis.

We must remember that society's social relationships and structures are not natural in form. They are also not static, but evolve over time, influenced by cultural, historical, and political changes, and must be continually reassessed to ensure they remain equitable and just. These institutional structures are not natural but are the products of history, culture, policy, and politics, typically reinforced or compelled through law and by governing entities. The individual (as well as the politics and

---

recognize and adapt to the possibilities of change. These groups have been referred to as vulnerable, a tactic that has successfully worked to activate and justify limited and targeted state action in a system where such action is generally seen as inappropriate intervention absent exceptional circumstances. One major problem with this particularized approach to vulnerability is that it undermines the potential power of the concept to achieve generalized structural reform while also obscuring the reality of universal vulnerability. This also illuminates a second major problem with a particularized approach. If the issue is discrimination and the remedy is inclusion in a fundamentally flawed or unjust institution, this will not represent much of a victory for the particular individual or group.

policies that affect the individual) should never be theorized as separate from the structural circumstances in which they are embedded.

Interestingly, the recognition and contextualizing or institutionalizing of a universal subject is also likely to provide the most extensive and practical benefits for particular individuals. State responsibility is greatly expanded beyond negative liberty models of individual rights or situations where there is a need to prevent discrimination. If our notions of state or collective (as well as individual) responsibility were shaped with a clear understanding of universal vulnerability and inevitable reliance on social institutions, state intervention would not be seen as only to be occasionally tolerated, but as necessary for individual and societal wellbeing. As a result, the position of any particular individual would be more clearly and justly assessed than it would be if they were perceived as independent and autonomous (and thus isolated and abandoned to mythical constructs of consent and contract). There are two additional important implications of Vulnerability Theory that affect how we understand the scope and extent of collective or governmental responsibility.

### 6.2.1.1 Reframing the individual within social structures

Since the foundational concept is the embodied individual, the template for the universally vulnerable subject would naturally span the life course, not be confined to only one stage or form of being. By contrast, the liberal legal subject is perceived as an adult, a fully functioning participant in some mythical social contract who is supposedly protected by the illusions of agency and independence. Those who fall outside of that construct are not perceived as entitled to or capable of enjoying the full benefits and protections of the preferred full legal subject. With Vulnerability Theory, the legal subject has been expanded to be inclusive of all stages and variations in the human condition. The expansion of the legal subject to encompass all stages of life underscores the need for a broader understanding of legal and political responsibilities.

*6.2.1.2 Implications for legal and political theory*

The second significant implication of the theory also is related to the idea of an expanded legal subject but focuses on the institutional arrangements that are central in a vulnerability analysis. Bringing in various life stages highlights the naturalness of relations of inequality, such as those that exist between parent and child. While inherently unequal, such relationships are not necessarily unjust; some are even necessarily unequal. However, it should be the responsibility of the governing bodies to regulate these relationships so as to promote fairness and prevent them from becoming sites of exploitation or abuse.

Lecture 4 on 'Inevitable Inequality' showed how unequal family relationships were not unique, but exemplary of many, if not most, social arrangements. Other examples included employer/employee, doctor/patient, and landlord/tenant. Concepts of equality, contract, and consent simply do not address the ways in which these ubiquitous asymmetric arrangements should be monitored in terms of the power, options, and resources they reflect. The glorification of some mythical autonomous individual in contemporary political culture has allowed theorists and politicians to avoid the hard questions about the need for governmental action implicit in these situations of inherent institutional inequality.

## 6.2.2 Biological mandates

The grounding of Vulnerability Theory in the physical body rather than resorting to aspirational abstractions is not merely a rhetorical device, but a deliberate strategy to underscore the corporeal constraints that shape our experiences, define our needs, and compel our relationships. It highlights that our vulnerabilities are not occasional or situational but constant and intrinsic, demanding ongoing and responsive engagement from both the state and society.

The mandate regarding governmental or collective responsibility that arises from this approach to what it means to be human is very different than the one that currently operates to severely curtail or constrain programmes and policy measures. Liberal restraint jealously guards the individual's autonomy and liberty. By contrast, a vulnerability approach would emphasize the biological and interactive or relation-dependent nature of the human condition. This would naturally lead to considering what governmental, social, legal, and ideological arrangements are essential for human and societal function and thriving. Such an inquiry must extend beyond material needs to encompass the emotional, psychological, and social dimensions of wellbeing, acknowledging that these too are critical to human flourishing. In exploring these mandates, we can see how they align with the broader social functions and roles necessary for individual and societal wellbeing.

As discussed in previous chapters, multiple social functions and roles are necessities for the wellbeing of the individual as well as the reproduction of society. These include the production of various essential goods and services, such as caretaking, education, housing, and healthcare, as well as systems for establishing economic and financial stability, security, and dispute resolution, but also the less tangible but equally important needs for belonging, purpose, and social trust. These intangible needs are often overlooked in traditional policy frameworks, yet they are foundational to social cohesion and individual wellbeing, providing the sense of community and shared purpose that is vital for a functioning society. It is these systems and institutions that form the backbone of a functioning society, ensuring that individuals are supported throughout the various stages of their lives. However, it is not enough for these institutions merely to exist; they must be dynamic and responsive, capable of adapting to the evolving needs of society.

Social institutions have been constructed around these and other essential needs, which serve as mechanisms of both distribution and normalization. They are the means through which society allocates resources and opportunities, but they are also the sites that can entrench existing power dynamics and inequalities. Once established, institutions must be effectively monitored to successfully function.

Institutional structures can be thought of as mediating entities that fulfil the state's responsibility to the individual while also operating to normalize and standardize the behaviour, expectations, and aspirations of the individuals acting within them. These structures, therefore, have a dual role: they not only provide the necessary support but also shape the societal norms and values that guide behaviour and interaction. The dual role of institutions – as providers of necessary support and as shapers of societal norms – makes them powerful tools for both preserving and transforming society.

While variations in institutional form are not only possible but are evident across cultures and throughout history, some functions are essential to the survival of the individual. These social institutions and relationships form the infrastructure of our day-to-day lives, and we rely on them, often without being conscious of doing so. Our reliance on these institutions is both a reflection of our vulnerability and a testament to the importance of a well-functioning social order. Figure 2.2 and accompanying text presented at the conclusion of Chapter 2 depict the symbiotic and complementary nature of these essential social arrangements.[3] It has become increasingly

---

[3] Referring to the example of what is referred to as the family/work conflict, what we can observe is that, when perceived as separate and unrelated, each institutional arrangement can be determined to operate according to a distinct set of values and norms (the family as private and altruistic, the market as public and efficient or competitive). There is a profound and consequential failure to see how these institutions actually facilitate or impede the functioning and success of other social institutions

clear that these institutional structures and mandates must also be designed to withstand and respond to large-scale challenges.

## 6.3 Collective crises

Global crises, such as the COVID-19 pandemic, the destructive effects of climate change, and the social dislocation and suffering resulting from pervasive economic and social inequality, reveal the inevitably common nature of embodied vulnerability, as well as the need for comprehensive and rigorous collective responses. These crises also reveal how important it is that government entities respond to vulnerability and dependency as a matter of routine by establishing effective bureaucratic mechanisms that are able to anticipate and plan for ways to adjust and respond to calamitous events, protecting both individuals and society.

A proactive approach to governance – one that anticipates vulnerabilities rather than merely reacting to crises – emerges not just as a policy choice but as an imperative to not only mitigate the impact of crises when they occur, but to ensure preparedness for future challenges. Unfortunately, all too often, governmental planning takes a more scattered, crisis-by-crisis approach, justifying this by reference to budgetary concerns and the need for austerity. Such a piecemeal and reactive stance often leaves a society more at risk in the future by failing to address the conditions that made a society susceptible to a crisis in the first place.

Also of significance are the political and sometimes legal obstacles in those systems that tend to prefer principles of

---

(the way that market norms have frustrated attempts to reform the family according to more egalitarian ideals). These institutions reflect human interactions and behaviour but are seldom the products of intentional and studied design. Instead, they tend to be the result of reactive politics, perhaps the products of crisis that provoked regulations out of perceived necessity, rather than deliberate planning.

individual over collective responsibility. As instructed by Vulnerability Theory, these obstacles are rooted in a misguided prioritization of individual autonomy over collective wellbeing, which hinder the development of effective policies that could better protect both individuals and society as a whole. Overcoming these obstacles requires a shift in legal and political paradigms, where the protection and promotion of collective welfare are recognized as central responsibilities of the state.

### 6.3.1 The US experience – individual over institutional

In the US, the pandemic exposed inadequacies in our political, social, economic, and healthcare systems. These inadequacies were not *new* but were exacerbated and brought into sharp relief by the crisis, revealing deep-seated structural flaws that have long been neglected. While the virus does not discriminate, the inadequate and fragile nature of the social welfare infrastructure meant that its impact was greatest on those with the fewest personal options, assets, and resources (those with the least resilience).

Court decisions and partisan politics encouraged individuals not to cooperate with preventive measures, such as masking, and vaccination rates were low by international standards. This lack of cooperation both reflects and deepens a broader crisis of trust and social empathy/bonds, where individualism and political polarization have undermined collective action, making it difficult to implement effective public health strategies. This lack of cooperation, fuelled by a toxic combination of misinformation, distrust, and political division, further undermined the response to the pandemic and exacerbated its effects.

Similar patterns of crisis response can be seen in environmental challenges, where systemic flaws again become apparent. Environmental changes have triggered some catastrophic reminders of our relation to and dependence upon ecological systems. These environmental crises, like the pandemic, make apparent the interconnectedness of human and ecological health, revealing how the degradation of natural systems directly impacts human wellbeing. These changes, which are becoming increasingly frequent and severe, serve as stark reminders of our vulnerability to forces beyond our control and our dependence on a healthy and stable environment. Heatwaves, fires, flooding, and pollution have affected neighbourhoods, agricultural production, and the economy. These events not only threaten physical safety and economic stability but also challenge or undermine the very foundations of social order, as communities are displaced, livelihoods destroyed, and social bonds frayed. These are not challenges that can be addressed by individuals in isolation.

The scale and complexity of these challenges demand coordinated and sustained governmental action. In the US, this type of comprehensive response would require the displacement of our individual rights discourse and the political and judicial recognition of our collective dependency on a sustainable and healthy ecosystem. This would require a theoretical and doctrinal re-evaluation of governmental responsibility to include the collective, including future generations over the asserted right of an individual.

Gross economic and social inequality also produces circumstances that harmfully affect the collective (as well as the individual) and are in need of sustained governmental response. Deepened by recent crises, these inequalities pose significant risks to the social fabric, undermining stability and cohesion. In this context, it is the body politic that is placed in danger, as inequality, exploitation, and marginalization foster not only dissatisfaction but suspicion about and distrust in a system that professes to be organized around a very different set of norms and values. This growing disillusionment further erodes social cohesion, complicating the implementation of collective solutions needed to address these challenges.

## 6.3.2 Vulnerability – mandate or imperative

It might be productive at this point to consider the distinction between a 'mandate' and an 'imperative'. This question between designations might also be framed as the difference between considering a crisis a moral or ethical dilemma or understanding it as presenting a situation that is existential in scope and implication. In the first instance, the collectively experienced crises addressed in the preceding section would be met with the creation of rules based on ethical or moral principles. Formal requirements would be imposed by an external authority, and (hopefully) followed out of obligation and respect for the rule of law. Response through the creation of mandates would certainly recognize that these crises were significant and deserving of governmental attention. However, should we not wish to convey an even greater sense of urgency and necessity given the potentially dire nature of these impending collective catastrophes?

The idea that these (and other) collective crises are actually existential in nature and scope may more accurately and effectively convey the underlying necessity of action to avert catastrophe. In other words, existential imperatives arise from the recognition of the profound consequences of inaction, which is consistent with Vulnerability Theory's notion of injury from neglect. A shift from the more discretionary rule-based mandate to an existential imperative would highlight that the state's role is not just to enforce rules, but to proactively safeguard its citizens through vigilant and responsive governance.

In essence, the response to the vulnerable human condition must move beyond the negotiable to be understood as an existential necessity. The existential nature of these crises reflects the biological and social realities of human existence, making it imperative to effectively and comprehensively respond with those realities firmly in mind. This approach resonates with sociobiological and other theories that take embodiment and its implications seriously.[4] However, Vulnerability Theory goes beyond the imperatives imposed by the biological (embodiment) to also focus on the essential, but varied and distinct processes whereby governmental responses are developed. While theories such as that provided by sociobiology can provide valuable insights into the biological underpinnings of individual behaviour, Vulnerability Theory expands on this insight by emphasizing the corresponding essential societal task of constructing the social, political, and legal structures responsive to that biological reality. Our survival as a species depends not only on our biological adaptability but also on our ability to create and sustain institutions that are responsive to the complex and evolving needs of all individuals. This comprehensive approach, which integrates biological and social dimensions, offers a comprehensive framework for understanding the challenges we face as a society and the corresponding imperatives for action.

Perhaps what we need is an approach to law and policy based on an 'existential pragmatism', or 'pragmatic determinism', that would insist that rules and governmental responses must be intimately anchored in the existential realities/nature of human existence. This approach would discredit policies based on abstract, idealized conceptions of dignity, autonomy, or independence, which would then be seen as disconnected from the lived experiences of vulnerable individuals.

Ignoring human vulnerability and dependency *fundamentally* and *foundationally* limits our understanding of justice and equality. Such an oversight not only perpetuates existing injustices but also fails to address the deeper, systemic issues that arise from the neglect of the social and institutional implications of human vulnerability and fragility. We need

---

[4] See Edward O. Wilson, author of *Sociobiology: The New Synthesis* (Harvard University Press [1975] 2000), who stated that sociobiology is 'the systematic study of the biological basis of all social behavior'.

a radical, but pragmatic rethinking of the state's role. Rather than merely upholding theoretical rights or principles, the state must actively engage with the material and social realities of its citizens, creating conditions that foster resilience, security, and wellbeing. This shift involves not only providing essential services but also cultivating an environment where individuals and communities can thrive. Moving away from abstract liberal ideals of independence, autonomy, and self-sufficiency, this reimagined framework positions the state not as a distant or neutral arbiter but as an active participant in shaping the conditions necessary for a just and equitable society.

# Bibliography

## Books

Clarke, E.H. *Sex in Education, or, A Fair Chance for the Girls* (J.R. Osgood and Company 1873).

Fineman, M.A. *The Neutered Mother, the Sexual Family and Other Twentieth Century Tragedies* (Routledge 2014).

Harvey, D. *A Brief History of Neoliberalism* (Oxford University Press 2005).

Hayek, F.A. *The Road to Serfdom* (Routledge 1944).

Hayek, F.A. *Law, Legislation and Liberty, Volume 2: The Mirage of Social Justice* (Routledge 1976).

Hobbes, T. *Leviathan* (J.C.A. Gaskin, ed.) (Oxford University Press [1651] 2008).

Hoff, J. *Law, Gender, and Injustice: A Legal History of US Women* (NYU Press 1991).

Ibsen, H. *A Doll's House* (Dover Publications [1879] 1992).

Kessler-Harris, A. *Out to Work: A History of Wage-Earning Women in the United States* (Oxford University Press 1982).

Locke, J. *Second Treatise of Government: An Essay Concerning the True Original, Extent and End of Civil Government* (R.H. Cox, ed.) (Wiley-Blackwell 2014).

Merton, R.K. *Social Theory and Social Structure* (Free Press 1968).

Moynihan, D.P. *Family and Nation* (Harcourt 1986).

Ritter, G. *The Constitution as Social Design: Gender and Civic Membership in the American Constitutional Order* (Stanford University Press 2006).

Rousseau, J.-J. *Emile: or On Education*, 1st ed. (Penguin Classics 2007).

Shilling, C. *The Body and Social Theory* (SAGE Publications 2012).

Wilson, E.O. *Sociobiology: The New Synthesis* (Harvard University Press [1975] 2000).

## Chapters in edited volumes

Fineman, M.A. 'Reasoning from the Body: Universal Vulnerability and Social Justice' in C. Dietz, M. Travis, and M. Thomson (eds), *A Jurisprudence of the Body* (Springer 2020) 17–34.

Fineman, M.A. and Allard, S.W. 'Vulnerability, the Responsive State, and the Role of Religion' in H. Springhart and G. Thomas (eds), *Exploring Vulnerability* (Vandenhoeck & Ruprecht 2017) 81–99.

## Journals

Bernstein, D.E. 'Lochner's Feminist Legacy' (2003) 101 *Michigan Law Review* 1960.

Brown, K. '"Vulnerability": Handle with Care' (2011) 5(3) *Ethics and Social Welfare* 313–21.

Fineman, M. 'Cracking the Foundational Myths' (2000) 8(1) *American Journal of Gender, Social Policy, and the Law* 12–29.

Fineman, M.A. 'The Nature of Dependencies and Welfare Reform' (1996) 36 *Santa Clara Law Review* 287.

Fineman, M.A. 'The Inevitability of Dependency and the Politics of Subsidy' (1998) 9 *Stanford Law and Policy Review* 89.

Fineman, M.A. 'The Vulnerable Subject and the Responsive State' (2010) 60 *Emory International Law Review* 251–75.

Fineman, M.A. '"Elderly" as Vulnerable: Rethinking the Nature of Individual and Societal Responsibility' (2012) 20 *Elder Law Journal* 71–111.

Fineman, M.A. 'Vulnerability and Inevitable Inequality' (2017) 4(3) *Oslo Law Review* 133–49.

Fineman, M.A. 'Vulnerability and Social Justice' (2019) 53 *Valparaiso Law Review* 341–65.

Fineman, M.L. 'Images of Mothers in Poverty Discourses' (1991) 274(2) *Duke Law Journal* 274–95.

Fineman, M.L. 'Masking Dependency: The Political Role of Family Rhetoric' (1995) 81 *University of Virginia Law Review* 2181.

Novak, W.J. 'The Myth of the "Weak" American State' (2008) 113(3) *The American Historical Review* 752–72.

Van Parijs, P. 'Social Justice and the Future of the Social Economy' (2015) 86(2) *Annals of Public and Cooperative Economics* 191–7.

## Reports

Moynihan, D.P. *The Negro Family: The Case for National Action* (Office of Planning and Research, United States Department of Labor 1965). https://web.stanford.edu/~mrosenfe/Moynihan's%20The%20Negro%20Family.pdf. Accessed September 26, 2024.

United Nations Children's Fund (UNICEF). *Early Childhood Development: UNICEF Vision for Every Child* (UNICEF 2023). https://www.unicef.org/media/145336/file/Early%20Childhood%20Development%20-%20UNICEF%20Vision%20for%20Every%20Child.pdf. Accessed September 26, 2024.

United Nations Department of Economic and Social Affairs, Division for Social Policy and Development. *Social Justice in an Open World: The Role of the United Nations*, UN Doc. ST/ESA/305 (2006). https://www.un.org/esa/socdev/documents/ifsd/SocialJustice.pdf. Accessed September 26, 2024.

## Websites and online

Encyclopaedia Britannica. 'Slave Codes' (n.d.) *Encyclopaedia Britannica*. https://www.britannica.c/topic/slave-code. Accessed September 26, 2024.

Encyclopedia.com. 'Liberal Democracy' (n.d.) *Encyclopedia.com*. https://www.encyclopedia.com/in/legal-and-p-magazines/lib-dem. Accessed September 26, 2024.

Feminism and Legal Theory Project, Emory University Law School's MacMillan Library. https://library.law.emory.edu/collections/feminism-and-legal-theory.html. Accessed September 26, 2024.

Fineman, M.A. 'What Vulnerability Theory Is and Is Not' (2021) *Vulnerability and the Human Condition Initiative*. https://scholarblogs.emory.edu/vulnerability/2021/02/01/is-and-is-not/. Accessed September 26, 2024.

HeinOnline. 'Women and the Law (Peggy) database' (n.d.) *HeinOnline*. https://libguides.heinonline.org/women-and-the-law. Accessed September 26, 2024.

Moyers, B. 'The Vanishing Family: Crisis in Black America' (1986) CBS television broadcast, January 25, transcript on file at University of Miami Law Review. Accessed September 26, 2024.

New York Times. 'The Position of Woman' (1908) *New York Times*, February 26. https://timesmachine.nytimes.com/timesmachine/1908/02/26/104797572.html?pageNumber=6. Accessed September 26, 2024.

Oxford Dictionaries. 'social contract' (2016) *Oxford English Dictionary*. https://www.oed.com/dictionary/social-contract_n?tab=etymology-paywall#21924478. Accessed September 26, 2024.

Oxford Languages. 'Generative' (n.d.) *Oxford English Dictionary*. www.oed.com/dictionary/generative_adj. Accessed September 26, 2024.

Trinity Lectures. 'Vulnerability, Justice, and the Human Condition' (n.d.) *Vimeo*. https://vimeo.with/showcase/9966989. Seminar 1: *Reasoning from the Body*, October 11, 2022; Seminar 2: *Vulnerability and Social Justice*, November 1, 2022; Seminar 3: *Injury – Beyond Equality and Discrimination*, November 22, 2022; Seminar 4: *Responding to Inevitable Inequality*, December 13, 2022. Accessed September 26, 2024.

Vobejda, B. 'Clinton Signs Welfare Bill Amid Division' (1996) *The Washington Post*, August 23. https://www.washingtonpost.com/wp-srv/politics/special/welfare/stories/wf082396.htm. Accessed September 26, 2024.

## Legal cases

*Bosley v McLaughlin*, 236 US 385 (1915).
*Bradwell v Illinois*, 83 US (16 Wall.) 130 (1873).
*Goesaert v Cleary*, 335 US 464 (1948).
*Hawley v Walker*, 232 US 718 (1914).
*Lochner v New York*, 198 US 45 (1905).

*Miller v Wilson*, 236 US 373 (1915).
*Mueller v Oregon*, 208 US 412 (1908).

## Other

*US Constitution*, Amendment XIX (1920).
Wiesel, E. as quoted in *US News and World Report*, October 27, 1986.

## Additional Vulnerability Theory resources (by M.A. Fineman)

### Books

*The Autonomy Myth: A Theory of Dependency* (The New Press 2004). Published in Japan as 作品社 (Sakuhinsha Publishing Company 2008).
*The Neutered Mother, The Sexual Family, and Other Twentieth Century Tragedies* (Routledge Press 1995). Published with updates in Japan as 学陽書房 Gakuyo (Shobo Publishing Company 2003).

### Edited volumes

*Law and Structuring Individual and Institutional Responsibility: Beyond Equality* (with Laura Spitz) (Routledge 2023).
*Privatization, Vulnerability, and Social Responsibility: A Comparative Perspective* (with U. Andersson and T. Mattsson) (Routledge 2017).
*Vulnerability and the Legal Organization of Work* (with J. Fineman) (Routledge 2018).
*Vulnerability and the Organization of Academic Labor* (with G. Ferris) (Routledge 2024).
*Vulnerability: Reflections on a New Ethical Foundation for Law and Politics* (with A. Grear) (Ashgate Press 2013).

### Journals

'Beyond Equality and Discrimination' (2020) 73 *SMU Law Review Forum* 51.

'Beyond Identities: The Limits of an Anti-discrimination Approach to Equality' (2012) 92 *Boston University Law Review* 1713.

'Equality and Difference – The Restrained State' (2015) 66 *Alabama Law Review* 609.

'Homeschooling the Vulnerable Child' (2016) 46(1) *University of Baltimore Law Review* (with G. Shepherd).

'Populations, Pandemics, and Politics' (2021) 21 *International Journal of Discrimination and the Law* 3.

'Rights, Resilience, and Responsibility' (2022) 71 *Emory Law Journal* 1435.

'The Significance of Understanding Vulnerability: Ensuring Individual and Collective Well-Being' (2023) 36(4) *International Journal for the Semiotics of Law – Revue internationale de Sémiotique juridique* 1371–83.

'The Vulnerable Subject' (2008) 20 *Yale Journal of Law and Feminism* 1.

'Universality, Vulnerability, and Collective Responsibility' (2021) 16(1) *Les ateliers de l'éthique/The Ethics Forum. Special Issue: 'After Covid': Ethical, Political, Economic and Social Issues in a Post-Pandemic World.*

'Vulnerability and LGBT Youth' (2014) 23(2) *Temple Political and Civil Rights Law Review* 307–30.

'Vulnerability as a Basis for Justice and Equality in the Nordic Countries – Afterword: Vulnerability and Resilience' (2013) 36 *Retfaerd* 84 (The Nordic Journal of Law and Justice).

'Vulnerability in Law and Bioethics' (2020) 30 *Journal of Health Care for the Poor and Underserved* 52.

# Index

References to figures appear in *italic* type. References to footnotes show both the page number and the note number (149n1).

## A

anti-discrimination
  and complementary social identities 88n20
  essential for a just society 100
  use of demographic categories 23–4
autonomy
  and collective responsibility 34–5n4
  and distribution of economic growth 66
  government action as instrusion 61, 63
  the idealized legal subject 2–3, 42–4
  and resistance to vulnerability as universal 37n9
  and state responsibility to basic needs 29
  unrealistic expectations of independence and rationality 31–2, 91

## C

competent rights holder 43–4

## D

dependency
  collective or societal debt 78
  derivative dependency 46, 77–8, 91n1
  early conceptualization of Vulnerability Theory 78–80
  examples of social policy responses 26
  as expression of vulnerability 44–5
  the family is not sufficient 46–7
  inherent in the human condition 46, 47n28
  and injury 77–82
  'natural' dependence of women 13
  overlooked by feminism 10–11
  as universal 11, 80–1
  and vulnerability 7–8

## E

economics
  burden of institutional failure allocated to individual 103
  efficiency and exploitation model 81n11
  fair and compassionate distribution of economic growth 64–7
  individual's freedom to consume 62–3
  Porsche preference 81n11
  the rational actor ignores the dependent body 43–4.
  *See also* neoliberalism
educational system
  and dependency 46
  institutional approach and governing collective organizations the 37
  as recipient of economic growth 103
  and resilience 68, 69–70
  social institution 113
  and social justice 85

embodiment
  and dependency 58
  embodied vs embedded
    vulnerability 50, *51*
  implications and
    limitations 84n15
  significance in Vulnerability
    Theory 29, 31, 33, 33, 39
  and the universal (vulnerable)
    legal subject 92
  and vulnerability 56–7, 92, 106
equality
  achieved by feminist legal
    reform 21–2
  anti-discrimination analysis 23–4
  as construct that limits change 2
  defining
  is opportunity distribution vs
    outcomes 64–5n18
  may create obstacles 100–1
  as overarching aspiration
    90, 91n1
  paradox of 19–21
  as protection against intrusion on
    autonomy 61
  as qualified concept 11–13
  rethinking ideas about family
    functioning 25–8
  sensitivity to gender differences
    needed 22–3. *See also* fictitious
    equality; gender equality;
    inevitable inequality

## F

the family
  cannot care for all
    vulnerability 28–9
  caretaking as non-monetary
    subsidy 80–1
  and dependency 46–7
  in feminist legal reform 4
  and inevitable inequality 104
  institutional approach
    and governing collective
      organizations 37
  privatization of the collective
    debt of care 78–9
  providing welfare
    cycles of dependency 77
  rethinking ideas about
    functioning 25–8
  as social institution
    an assumed institution 24
    state's involvement in
      regulating 14
Feminism and Legal Theory
  Project 76n5
feminist legal reform
  *Bradwell v Illinois* (1872) 15–16
  equality achieved 21–2
  equality as qualified concept
    11–13
  equality in an unequal world
    22–3
  and the family and the corporeal
    body 4
  the gendered constitutional and
    legal subject 14–21
  legally relevant gender
    differences 21
  *Muller v Oregon* (1908) 16–18, 19
  public and private spheres of life
    13–21
fictitious equality 101
Friedman, Martha 84–5

## G

gender
  effect of discrimination
    protection 63
  and institutional reform 4
  intersecting identities
    unjustly 103–4
gender equality
  the equality of women 11n2
  *Muller v Oregon* (1908) 16–18, 19
  *Reed v Reed* (1971) 21
  requires more complex
    framework 10–11

## H

Hayek, F. A. 62–3n17, 84–5
Hobbes, Thomas 16n9, 31n1

# INDEX

## I

inevitable inequality
  and children 101–2
  equality as unjust objective 101
  and the family 104
  inequality of fundamental social relationships 55, 100n10
  Institutional and infrastructural power 98–105
  state responsibility and institutional construction
  Authoritative or despotic power 96–7
  structuring institutional arrangements 95–6
  the unstable individual 93–5
  vulnerability and dependency as state must be recognized as state responsibility 7–8
injury
  and dependency 77–82
  failure of state to act 6–7, 92, 96–7
  and the family institution 79
  and indifference 83–6, 88
  Individual and collective harm 75–7
  negative rights vs positive rights 72–3
  the social contract 72–4, 73n2
  and social debt 76
  state intervention as 6–7, 84–5
  and state responsibility 82–9
  still face paradigm 81–2
institutionalizing the individual
  approach to the body 107–8
  biological mandates 112–15
  collective crises 115–17
  and discrimination concerns 109
  future considerations 8–9
  implications for legal and political theory 112
  mandate vs imperative 118–20
  reframing the individual within social structures 111–12
  social and political implications 108–15

institutions and interdependence 47–52

## L

labour
  caretaking produces and preserves society 11, 78–81
  and distribution of economic growth 66
  in the family 24
  and fictitious equality 101
  gender and legislation 16–20
  institutional approach 37
  and welfare 62–3n17
the legal subject
  the gendered 14–21
  the liberal (idealized) subject and autonomy 2–3, 42–4
  replacing the liberal legal subject with the vulnerable subject 68
  the universal (vulnerable) legal subject 23, 44–7, 57, 75, 92–3
liberalism 6, 41n19, 50, 100
libertarianism 6, 61n13–14, 73–4
liberty
  constitutional principle 12–13
  as construct that limits change 2, 29
  and independence – ignoring the body 42–4
  no redistribution 74
  as protection against intrusion on autonomy 61
  state intervention as presumptively injurious 6
  unrealistic expectations of the individual 91
  unrealistic notions of 31–2
  of women limited by the state 17, 27
Locke, John 3n5, 11n2, 16n9, 31–2n1

## M

Merton, Robert
  theory of the middle range 1–2

## N

neoliberalism
  the market as part of societal wellbeing 87
  unrealistic notions of liberty and autonomy 31–2
  and welfare dependency 62–3n17
Nordic countries
  paternity leave 26
normative theory 73–4, 75

## R

reasonable man trope 43
religion 37
resilience 45, 54–5, 57n5, 68, 69–70, 106
Rousseau, Jean-Jacques 3n5, 11n2, 16n9

## S

the social contract 11n2, 16n9, 16n9, 49, 72–3, 73n2, 74, 86
social institutions
  burden of institutional failure allocated to individual 103
  and derivative dependency 46
  devises individual identities 103
  mechanism to distribute benefits 102–3
  and relationships 69–70
  responsibility for distribution spread over 103. *See also* educational system; the family
social justice
  addressing the abdication of state responsibility 88–9
  collective conception of 61, 61–2n14, 64–7, 64–7
  defining 58–60, 61
  defining egalitarian 63–5n18e
  difficulty of achieving a truly collection approach in current thinking 53–4
  in economic terms 62
  impacted by definitions of vulnerability 36
  the individual and conceptions of justice 61–7
  individualism 61, 61–2, 62–3
  and individual restraint 65, 65n20
  questions from a vulnerability perspective 70–1
  safety nets 63
  as universal 5–6
  and Vulnerability Theory, 67–70. *See also* United Nations
state action
  current failures in fulfilling its responsibility 47–8
  inaction as appropriate in relation to liberty or autonomy rights 74
  no redistribution 74
  inconsistent with the wellbeing of individuals 3
state responsibility
  and authoritative or despotic power 96–7
  effects of abdication 44
  evading responsibility by creating social institutions 102
  and indifference 83–6
  institutional and infrastructural power 98–105

## T

theory of the middle range 1–2

## U

2023 UNICEF analysis 83n13
United Nations
  'Social Justice in an Open World' report 54, 59–60, 61–2, 64–5, 65, 66, 67
the universal body
  based in reality not unrealistic expectations 31–2
  and collective responsibility 34, 36, 61
  the corporeal body as foundational to Vulnerability Theory 2
  and dependence 5, 44–7

# INDEX

developmental nature of 39–42
as foundational to Vulnerability Theory 5, 28
ignoring the body for liberty and independence 42–4
requires a different analysis, 33–4, *51*
responding to historical injustices vs vision beyond discrimination 40–1
US Constitution 11n2, 22–3, 54

## V

Van Parijs, Philippe 63–5n18
vulnerability
  as central to society and institutions
  the ontological body 5
  as continuum of variations 106
  defining 55–6n1, 55–7
  defining vulnerability 54–5
  and dependency as state must be recognized as state responsibility 7–8
  redefining 36–7
  the unstable individual 93–5
  'vulnerable children' an oxymoron 57–8n4
  the vulnerable subject in childhood 57
Vulnerability Theory
  democratic state to construct a just society 37–8
  distributional aspect of institutions and interdependence 50, *52*
  'existential pragmatism' or 'pragmatic determinism' 28–30
  first principle of 38
  focus is on the whole society 92
  and institutional analysis 23–4, 37
  institutional vs systemic approach 4
  policy and state responsibilities not individual rights 54–5
  redefining the baseline of state responsibility 40–1
  and resilience 68–9
  and the responsive state 29
  and social institutions and relationships 69–70. *See also* embodiment; social justice; the universal body

## W

Wiesel, Elie 7, 83
Wilson, Edward O. 84n15

www.ingramcontent.com/pod-product-compliance
Lightning Source LLC
Chambersburg PA
CBHW071716020426
42333CB00017B/2292